LUGGY

LUGGY

THE AUTOBIOGRAPHY OF PAUL STURROCK

PAUL STURROCK WITH BILL RICHARDS

FOREWORD BY WALTER SMITH OBE

First published by Pitch Publishing, 2015

Pitch Publishing

A2 Yeoman Gate

Yeoman Way

Durrington

BN13 3QZ

www.pitchpublishing.co.uk

ISBN 978-1-78531-045-4

Typesetting and origination by Pitch Publishing

Printed by TJ International, Cornwall, UK

Contents

Walter Smith OBE – former Scotland, Rangers and Everton manager

I HAVE known Paul Sturrock from when he came in as a rookie wannabe footballer at Dundee United in the 1970s and have watched his playing and managerial career flourish ever since.

So, it is a genuine pleasure to be asked to contribute to his life story which has seen Paul win trophies and league titles with Dundee United, caps for Scotland and promotions as a manager both north and south of the border.

It is no surprise to me and no accident either that Paul has earned the reputation as one of the most successful managers and coaches outside of the Premier League in England. I remember Paul or 'Luggy' as he became better known, as a very keen youth player, one of several that United's manager Jim McLean had brought to Tannadice.

It was obvious that Paul had the drive and ambition to become a first-team player, and his willingness to learn and improve was evident from the word go.

That he has achieved so much in the game is a testament to his work ethic and attention to detail and what he was being taught and told.

Paul is a football man through and through, and the discipline and professionalism was learnt early on at Dundee United under Jim McLean. But it is to Paul's credit that he was willing to go that extra yard.

It is fair to say that Paul was probably not the finished article when he burst into the first team, but through hard work and extra training with the coaches at Tannadice, he very quickly became an outstanding striker and established himself in an excellent Dundee United squad.

Paul had a great attitude and was a model pupil, which as any coach will tell you, is rewarding both for player and coach.

As a player, Paul clearly relished a challenge and worked his socks off with myself and Gordon

Wallace in extra training and was straining at the leash to bring his left foot more into play.

He realised that we were working with him in extra training not for the good of our own health, but to help add another dimension to his forward play, which we achieved.

Although Paul was personally ambitious to turn himself into a better player, he was also extremely loyal to Dundee United, despite the interest of several bigger clubs, both in Scotland and in England.

He has said on record that he could not have been happier anywhere else, than at Tannadice, where he stayed for 16 years as a player and five years as a coach and latterly as manager.

One-club footballers are a rarity, particularly, when as an outstanding striker which Paul was, he could have made more money elsewhere.

But then, he was achieving so much at Dundee United at the time winning League Cups and championships and reaching European finals, so it suited Paul, who was a huge part and presence of the team's success. That applied to most of the United squad where individual talent, of which Paul was one, turned the side into an effective unit, as their record at that time clearly proves.

Paul, perhaps, was unlucky to be playing at a time when Scotland already had two very good strikers, in Kenny Dalglish and Steve Archibald. Otherwise he would have won more caps than he did.

That would be a regret to anybody, to say you're a better player than Kenny Dalglish who was one of the best players anywhere, never mind Scotland.

But Paul never gave up trying and I think it was that attitude which ensured he was always involved in the Scotland scene. He was also a very good character to have around the first team.

Through all the years I've known him, particularly early on as a young striker, I can honestly say that no-one worked harder to rise to a higher level as a player.

He also brought that same level of intensity to his coaching and later managerial career.

Paul was always working hard in coaching even in his early to mid-twenties and he made no secret of the fact that he wanted to get into management once his footballing days were over.

Paul's work ethic ensured that he would give it a good go, and, in fact, he has achieved a lot more than that as a coach and manager.

He worked really hard to achieve that level of ability as a player and did not let his own standards drop, which is precisely what he did as a coach and manager.

He accepts everything as a challenge and wherever he has managed and coached, no matter what the situation he finds himself in.

There's no doubt in my mind that Paul Sturrock is an outstanding manager in what is a difficult environment to be successful.

Looking back on my years at Dundee United, it was a very good time to be there and people like Paul made it all the more enjoyable and memorable.

Harry Redknapp
Tribute

I'VE KNOWN Paul for many years now, mainly through Jocky Scott and Gordon Wallace and have followed his career ever since. Obviously I knew him as an outstanding player with Scotland and Dundee United.

In his playing career Paul was unlucky that Kenny Dalglish was around otherwise he would have won an awful lot more Scotland caps than he did.

He played in a really good team up in Scotland and was a terrific footballer but no player would displace Kenny Dalglish in his prime.

As a manager, I've also watched his career blossom and I like the way his teams play the game.

We were rival managers when Paul was at Southampton and I was with Portsmouth for that short spell.

Our two sides played against each other down at St Mary's and we got to know each other again then.

If I was able to help Paul out with a loan player then I would and I did.

Paul's main attribute as a coach is first and foremost that he is a football man and knows the game.

He's been brought up around good coaches and managers up in Scotland and he has a fantastic understanding of the game.

There is no magic formula to the game – it's about good players and getting the best out of them.

He prepares his teams well and gets to know the strengths and weaknesses of his players and strives to get the best out of them.

And that is something Paul does well as his success rate of winning championships with his various clubs shows.

When you consider that Paul is having two things to manage in his career – his illness and football teams – I think that shows his courage and also his deep love of the game.

Naturally, I wish Paul every success at Yeovil Town and I will keep in touch with him and I'll go down to watch a game there, I'll enjoy that.

Introduction

I AM writing this book as a true account of my life – to date – in the game that I love, the characters I have met along the way who have inspired, influenced and shaped my career in football and also to put the record straight on a few issues.

I include the highs and lows of a career in football that spans over 40 years since, some great successes as a player with Dundee United and Scotland, and later as a promotion-winning manager both north and south of the border.

Inevitably, a few of my observations on events over the years will no doubt upset a few readers, but, hopefully, what follows will enlighten and entertain the most important players in the game – the fans.

I was minded to put pen to paper before now but was prompted by the number of people, whether supporters at one of my former clubs or just casual inquiries asking 'what are you up to now, Luggy, isn't it time you either got back into management or write your life story'.

Well, as the phrase goes 'be careful what you wish for' as I won't be leaving anything out – it's been quite a journey for a wee Scot who didn't know whether he would be able to make a living from the game, but always knew he wanted to try.

I am also in a good place right now, both personally and geographically, and that is thanks to the loving relationship I have with my partner of several years, Andrea.

We live together in a small village in south-east Cornwall, Menheniot, where Andrea and myself are leading the good life, fruit and vegetable growing and keeping horses in our stables.

It is our rock-solid relationship and the terrific community life in the village which keeps me anchored in the West Country and I cannot imagine living anywhere else.

This is the real deal.

But it's time to turn from the present and leaf through my back pages, so here goes.

Luggy

FOOTBALL has been my life pretty much since I was old enough to walk and beneath the now stockier and older version I'm still the same skinny kid who practised on his own for hours kicking the ball with both feet against a wall.

I still strive to improve as a manager and coach just as I was encouraged to do as a young player at Tannadice and that burning ambition to bring success to the great clubs I have been fortunate to have managed has not been extinguished.

I have enjoyed fantastic moments both as a striker for my beloved Arabs and, of course, had the honour of representing Scotland in two World Cups.

It may sound a cliché to say that I haven't lost my enthusiasm despite personal setbacks and health problems but it is the literal truth. I still remember vividly the moment when I was informed by a specialist that I was suffering from Parkinson's disease just as I was about to take over at a Premier League club.

Being told I had Parkinson's was a devastating blow not just for my health but for my future. It's like the little boy in the sweetie shop having had a taste of something nice, only to have the door slammed shut on you.

I know for a fact that my illness has cost me the chance to manage at a few football clubs whenever a vacancy has arisen.

Strange that, when you consider I'd already won promotions with St Johnstone, Plymouth Argyle, Sheffield Wednesday, Swindon Town and steered Southend United to a Wembley final, as well as a spell as boss of Premier League side, Southampton.

But I'd overcome disappointments, before, like when I was overlooked for the Dundee United manager's job when it was clear to everyone but the board that I was the best man for the post.

But there's nothing I can do about that now except wonder what difference I might have made in the hot seat when Dundee United were flying.

I was very upset, too, at being left on the substitutes' bench for the 1982 World Cup finals, although proud and elated to play for my country in the 1986 World Cup.

But you bounce back or give up, don't you? Well, I'm no quitter and my love for the game and self-belief saw me through.

But I have nothing but great affection and respect for Jim McLean whom I rate up there with the fantastic Sir Alex Ferguson as a tactical genius.

However, it still rankles as at that time the Arabs were a brilliant side, winning trophies in Scotland and feared around Europe and I had contributed in no small measure, firstly as a striker and then a youth and first-team coach at Tannadice.

I did get to manage Dundee United but only after I had taken over the reins at St Johnstone, with whom I won my first promotion and helped keep the side in the top flight of the Scottish league system.

As much as I loved Dundee United, I am forever grateful for being given the chance to manage St Johnstone as my own man under an enlightened and supportive chairman, Geoff Brown.

It was a great learning curve and allowed me to stamp my own authority, managing in my own right.

Another painful memory comes from when I went back to my other great love – Argyle – for a second stint as manager and could not arrest their decline, for reasons outside of my control as I shall go on to explain.

That still leaves a sour taste in my mouth and I don't think the Green Army have been told the full story on that sorry chapter in the club's history.

As I stated earlier, my main reason for writing my life story is to set straight a few misconceptions and thank the supporters at all the clubs I have been lucky enough to either play for or manage for their good wishes.

I have enjoyed a terrific relationship with the supporters whose devotion to their respective clubs through thick and thin never fails to astonish and move me and helps to balance the scales against those in the game for whom I have no time for at all.

They know who they are and so will you by the time you've finished this book.

'Ear We Go

I N CASE you were wondering just why I insisted on calling my book 'Luggy' and not Paul Sturrock, let me explain.

I felt that like Paul Gascoigne is equally well known by his nickname 'Gazza', and Sir Alex Ferguson is universally known as 'Fergie' I am just as comfortable and happy to be called 'Luggy' as Paul Whitehead Sturrock, which is my full name.

Well, the origin of me being awarded that moniker goes back to my days as a youngster at Tannadice and it happened like this.

The nickname of 'Luggy', which I've had throughout my football career, refers to someone with big or sticky-out ears, well in Scotland it does, and I was awarded the tag when I first signed on as a youth player at Dundee United. Talk about the school of hard knocks – if I had any delusions of grandeur, they were swiftly shattered and in a painful manner.

It was my first day at Tannadice and I was dead keen to impress and went to get my kit which was in the boot room in the first-team changing room.

I knocked and was greeted by silence and none-too-friendly stares by the senior pros.

'Who the fuck are you and what are you doing here?' asked one of the players, talking on behalf of his team-mates.

I was stunned, of course, but replied: 'My name is Paul, Paul Sturrock and I have come to get my boots and tracksuit.'

'Well that's not how it's done here – what you do is go back out, knock on the first-team door and when we grant you entry, you crawl on all fours into the boot room, get your kit and fuck off out again.

'Got it?'

I was still raw and young compared to these guys but managed to splutter: 'I'm not doing that.'

The reply was swift and menacing: 'Oh, is that fucking right?' It was not so much a question as a lead up to the next lesson of my place on the Tannadice totem pole.

The door slammed shut and they basically gave me a slapping so there would be no further misunderstanding, as it were.

So, despite my initial resistance to their request, I needed the kit and so I did as I was told and knocked on the door and went in on all fours and my path was left unhindered.

After the training session and having showered and washed my hair, Andy Rolland who was then the bearer of the nickname 'Luggy' and clearly didn't like it much, saw his chance of diverting it to me and cried out to all and sundry: 'Look at the size of yon kid's ears!

'That's it from now his name is "Luggy", and it has stuck with me ever since.

Even though, now I've filled out a wee bit and my lugs don't stick out like they did!

Anyway, before all that happened, some background on my Scottish roots and my family history.

The Early Years

I WAS born in Ellon Parish Hospital, Aberdeenshire, in October 1956 and my father's family hail from Peterhead and my mother from a small fishing village called Boddam, which was a stone's throw from Peterhead.

My dad's name was George, mum Wilma and my siblings were Gail and Blair.

Sadly, my brother I never got to know as he died aged just 18 months old which was a tragic loss to my parents. However, his name lives on through my eldest boy, Blair, who has also made a career for himself as a professional footballer and who is also a very good golfer.

Gail, who is six years younger than me, has done well for herself, too, and is a pit boss with one of the big casinos in the Manchester area. She must have inherited her gambling instincts and prowess from my dad, who was a genius at cards and dominoes.

I'm sorry to say that he didn't always heed his own advice when it came to money, but my upbringing certainly helped me become self-reliant and astute when it came to financial dealings.

My parents split up when I was around 15 years old and dad remained with me in Scotland while mum and sister Gail moved south to Sunderland.

Mum is very well known and respected at Sunderland and has been a stalwart caterer in the club's boardroom for very many years.

As for my home life in Scotland it soon became obvious that dad was better at earning money than keeping it and without my mum around to oversee the household budget – that responsibility fell on my young shoulders.

So, I had to make sure that there was enough in the kitty to pay the bills; that's just how it was and shouldn't be seen as a criticism of my dad or my lot in life.

If anything, those roles of getting involved in running a house at an early age toughened and sharpened me up as at every football club I've managed, certainly in the early part of my career, I tried to make sure that everything was being run properly from the bottom to the top and knew who was responsible for what.

I like to get involved so that if stuff isn't going as well as it should, I know who to call.

Taking responsibility for others came early to me, then, and even before my parents' split, I was called upon to rescue dad from a tricky situation. I'd have been about 11 or 12, I suppose, when the Sturrock household was awoken in the middle of the night by one of my dad's workmates.

We were living in a railway house and the duty railway porter came pounding on our door, alarmed that he couldn't contact my dad who was supposed to be on duty in the signal box.

Dad was on duty – working as a signalman – but got worse for wear at one of the local hostelries before his nightshift.

In fact, he was practically unconscious in a room just off the signal box and unaware that the mail train from Inverness was awaiting the all clear to proceed, as the signals were on stop.

It took my mum, me and the by now panic-struck railway worker all our collective strength to get my dad compos mentis enough to show us which levers did what, so that the mail train could get through.

So, that was dad's claim to fame – holding up the night mail train for the best part of three-and-a-half hours – even though he knew little about the scary story.

Fortunately for my dad, in those days the trades union was strong and claimed dad had just passed out. He kept his job, although I'm certain he learnt from the experience.

Later on, my father moved to Sunderland to help my mother, who by that time had re-married, to keep an eye on my sister, who was fast becoming a bit of a tearaway, probably due to the change of circumstances.

Although, it might also have been a ruse to keep dad out of trouble, too.

But that was much later on and I was already established at Dundee United, under the unerring and unforgiving eyes of Jim McLean.

4

The Mighty Jim

DESCRIBING Jim McLean as a disciplinarian is only half the story, for although he ruled with a rod of iron, without his guidance and astute judgement I wouldn't have been half the player I was later to become.

You got on the wrong side of Jim at your peril as I was to find out.

But I'm getting ahead of myself and how I came to consider football as a career in the first place.

My dad, who passed away some years back, was firstly head baker at the Fisher's Hotel in Pitlochry, before he worked on the railway and although never a good enough footballer himself, he, like my mum, was very supportive of my career and offered me good advice when it came to my professional career.

There was no kids' football in Pitlochry aside from at school and so we used to play on a grassy area in the middle of a housing scheme.

So, our floodlights were the street lamps and we'd go home, get changed, have tea and play, basically, 25-a-side matches which would be reduced in numbers when parents would drive up and shout for their kid to get into the car.

You'd get down to five-a-side eventually.

I'd always wanted to be a footballer and when not playing against boys the same age or older, I would be kicking the ball against the big wall that belonged to the cinema that backed on to our house.

The road it was on was very rarely used in those days and so I could learn to trap and kick with both feet and I would spend hours there learning close control with a few mates.

One of the boys was playing for a team nearby and one day I went to watch him play, along with one of my other mates who had a car.

We would be about 14 or 15 years old and at this particular match, my mate's team, Grandtully Vale, only had 10 players and so it was a toss-up between yours truly, small and scrawny and my pal who was a big, sturdy lad, but who wore glasses like the bottom of a Coca-Cola bottle.

I think it was the spectacles that put the manager off and so I was picked to play on the wing and Billy my mate was on the bench. That was the start of something for me, I played the whole season for Grandtully Vale, eventually against men, not against people my own age.

I'd be about 15 and to be honest it was the best thing that ever happened to me as although I'd played for my school and my county against boys my own age, playing against men toughened me up.

I played for my local team – the Vale of Atholl – mainly because a few of my mates were with them and I scored a hatful of goals that season.

But I was playing amateur football regularly and that led to me being spotted by a Dundee United scout. I was playing for a team called Bankfoot Athletic, which was a few miles south of Pitlochry in Perthshire, but importantly it was for a side one level higher.

The way it was then, you went in by degree starting with amateurs, semi-pros and then professionals and the standard was excellent.

I was 16 then and I think from memory I scored about 50 goals that year and Jim McLean, who had signed several boys from Pitlochry – which is remarkable really as it is in the middle of nowhere – came to watch me playing for Bankfoot Juniors against Lochee Harp in the Tayside Junior League.

When you played in the Tayside Junior League, the city of Dundee comes into play, so that's the link there. Anyway, as a result, Jim wanted me and another lad to sign for United but he wanted me to sign an 'S' form, which is schoolboy terms and my dad wasn't too happy about, as it tied you to the club.

An amateur form doesn't, so although you are affiliated to the club, you can look around at others which my dad wanted for me, just in case.

Now, the manager of Bankfoot was also a talent scout for Dundee United and when Jim made it clear that he wanted to sign me, I was advised by the scout to tell him I was 16 and not 17 which I then was.

I was so desperate to become a footballer that I agreed and signed on for Dundee United as a 16-year-old which wasn't the truth.

My progress was rapid and a few months later I was on the Dundee United bench for a European tie against a Romanian side called Juil Petrosani and I got on for the last 15 minutes of the game.

All that I can remember about that period was that I was dubbed the youngest Scottish footballer ever to play in Europe. Supposedly, I had beaten Jim McLean's brother, Tommy, by about 50 days or thereabouts, but obviously I had been lying about my age, and I was agonising about what to do about it.

After confiding in the senior players, they told me to go and clear the air with the manager, as it was obvious I was in a dilemma and it needed resolving.

So, I had to face the music and remember, I was just a tenderfoot teenager, and Jim McLean was a massive man and a legend.

But I told Jim what the story was and he thundered 'you lied to me' and he immediately picked the phone up and told the manager of the team I had played for, who remember was his scout, he was sacking him on the spot for his part in the deception.

That's how much of a disciplinarian Jim was and it was harsh as the scout had discovered me and also Ray Stewart, who went on to play for West Ham and Scotland.

But he still got the sack, while I played the last six or seven games for United in the 1974/75 season, making my full debut against Rangers.

The Rise And Rise
Of Dundee United

I MADE a boys own start to my playing career for the Arabs, scoring our two goals in a 2-2 draw with Rangers.

I played up front alongside Andy Gray who later went on to play for Wolves and enjoy great success with Aston Villa.

Starting for United and scoring twice against the mighty Rangers was undoubtedly the kick-start to my football career. However, it was not plain sailing as for the next two seasons I was in and out of the first team as United were going through a bad time, around the period the Scottish top flight division was being reduced to 10 teams.

And, as chance would have it, both ourselves and our city neighbours and great rivals Dundee were in the bottom two.

The team who finished last was relegated to the tier below, the first division, and on the final day of the regular football season, we were playing Rangers at Ibrox, and Dundee were playing Celtic.

All we needed to do was to draw in order to survive the drop. Jim's brother Tommy was playing for Rangers, or rather he wasn't, and you could see his heart wasn't in it as he wanted United to stay up and as far as I can remember he didn't touch the ball in what ended in a 0-0 stalemate, so we were saved and Dundee were relegated.

From then on I became a regular in the United side and in the 1978/79 season we won the League Cup, the first trophy that Dundee United had ever won.

We beat Aberdeen, then coached and managed by Fergie, over two legs, the first ending goalless at Hampden Park.

It was agreed by the SFA and the finalists that the replay would be staged at Dens Park, Dundee's ground, so that both sets of supporters wouldn't have to travel to Glasgow, therefore cutting down on costs.

Aberdeen had shaded the first tie and were the favourites going into the replay, but United won 3-0 and I scored one of the goals, to help my side to silverware.

Although we were a middle of the road team in the league, the following season we went to the final again, this time against our city adversaries, Dundee, and as we didn't want to go to Hampden again, it was decided that we'd pick the venue on the toss of a coin.

Dundee won the toss but lost the final, with United prevailing again 3-0 and, of course, we had defended the trophy, which believe me, in a domestic tournament dominated by Rangers and Celtic, was a great achievement.

For the fans and us it was a great feeling gaining the bragging rights over Dundee who had been a top team in the sixties, with United taking over that mantle in the seventies and eighties.

The following season we reached the final again and played Rangers at Hampden Park and I believe, should have won the trophy again.

In a tightly-fought match, I thought I had won it for United, who were leading 1-0 at the time.

I remember that I beat the full-back, cut in from the left and smashed a shot into the top corner for a

2-0 lead. Only it wasn't to be as one of our defenders had been overlapping and although he ducked and didn't touch the ball, it was deemed he was in an offside position and the 'goal' was ruled out with Rangers going on to win the match 2-1 to take the trophy away from us.

We were all gutted as United deserved to make it a hat-trick of victories.

On such margins are issues decided but it didn't upset the Arabs' winning mentality as the next year, we won the 1982/83 league championship and that was an even greater achievement.

I have no hesitation in stating that was the best of the best for Dundee United in terms of personnel and further illustrated the tactical genius of Jim McLean and the talent in the team from outside the magic circle of supposed top sides.

Aberdeen had already won the championship twice, and so for us to win the title, too, was something special, as it broke up the duopoly previously the domain of the top two teams – Glasgow Rangers and Glasgow Celtic.

And, just as importantly, our new status confirmed Dundee United as not only one of the most successful sides in the UK, but also in Europe. We built up a fearsome reputation and defeated the likes of Roma, Werder Bremen, Monaco, Anderlecht, Lens, and Hajduk Split, and United had no sense of inferiority as our fitness, pace and fluidity made us formidable foes.

Beating Monaco, who were the richest club in Europe at that time, 5-2, on their own ground, was probably key to Dundee United shedding their corner-shop club reputation in terms of finance. Almost all of the squad which won the Scottish title had come through the youth ranks and that forged our family spirit and made United a team every footballer wanted to join.

In fact, if the referee hadn't been bribed in the European Cup semi-final, then Dundee United would have played Liverpool in the 1984 European Cup Final.

We took a 2-0 lead from Tannadice to Roma and the Italian crowd were hostile and pelted us with oranges and everything else they could lay their hands on, while their players were really aggressive and went on to win the game 3-0 to wipe out our advantage.

Roma's manager claimed we must have been on drugs in the first leg and he also came up with the genius stroke of telling his players that Jim McLean said there was no way that the Dundee United he had built would have lost a 2-0 lead. So with all that and our squad carrying injuries, in addition to having the referee on their side, the tie was tipped against us.

We found out about four years later that the referee, a French official called Michel Vautrot, had been tapped up by Roma and the final had been designated by UEFA to be played at the Stadio Olimpico.

Liverpool went on to beat Roma on penalties, but it should have been Dundee United playing the Reds in an Anglo-Scottish showpiece on May 30 1984, but we were denied the opportunity unfairly and it has stuck in our craw ever since.

I've recently contacted Michel Platini at UEFA stating our case and saying that it should be recognised and perhaps Dundee United's players should be awarded medals which would go some way to righting a wrong. But the UEFA president replied saying the timeframe was past and there was nothing he could do about it now.

That's sad as for Dundee United players to play in a European Cup Final would have been incredible and a vindication of the team Jim had built up and a recognition of not only his tactical genius but also the uniqueness of spirit and skill in the side, a squad of 17 or 18 mostly home-produced players that cost nothing like our rivals.

In fact, nothing will eclipse the achievement of Dundee United reaching a European Cup Final in my years at the club.

My playing career finished in 1989 and although there was the European Cup Final that should have been ours and not Roma's, my one big regret was that I played in five Scottish Cup finals and didn't win any of them.

During my time with Dundee United we had won two League Cup finals and also the Scottish League and appeared in a UEFA Cup Final, losing narrowly to an established top European side IFK Gothenburg 2-1 over two legs.

Gothenburg won the first tie in Sweden on May 6 1987 and we drew 1-1 at Tannadice a couple of weeks later with John Clark equalising to set up a fantastic final 30 minutes for the fans.

And it shouldn't be forgotten that we had beaten quality teams like Barcelona to reach the final. These were fantastic times.

It's important to point out, too, that this was the second great team that Jim had built, although the backbone remained of the players who had won the Scottish League title.

But it remains a personal regret that we weren't able to win a Scottish Cup final in my time with the club.

Shooting Star

MY STAR was in the ascendancy during United's glory years and one of my proudest moments came when I was named Scottish player of the year in 1982.

There were a number of English clubs interested in signing me as well as Celtic, who had already made several approaches, and also Rangers.

If Jim McLean had taken the manager's job at Ibrox he had been offered, chances are that David Narey and myself would have been his first signings and also the first high-profile Roman Catholics to play for Rangers, thus beating Maurice Johnston, who was later to sign for Gers, then managed by Graeme Souness in 1989.

But Jim didn't leave and so myself and team-mate and Scotland defender David both remained at Tannadice. But, although flattered by the interest, really, I had no great hankering to move to England such was my affection for Dundee United.

Everton and Stoke City were two of the teams in the race for my autograph, or to sign for either Celtic or Rangers, or Barcelona, then managed by Terry Venables, who wanted me having been impressed by my performances against them.

With all due respect to those great football sides, I was more than happy playing for my beloved Dundee United, and the feeling was mutual as they weren't prepared to release me in any case.

United were well ahead of their time in terms of tactics thanks to Jim McLean and his coaching staff and were among the first clubs to employ a psychologist, a nutritionist and sprint, weight and fitness trainers.

My role was as a playmaker/striker, holding up the ball as well as scoring my fair share of goals and the side's formation was fluid – we could adapt to a 4-5-1 system after switching from our more familiar 4-3-3.

For me, Jim McLean, had it not been for his terrible man-management style, would have gone down in football history as the genius I believe him to be, for he was head and shoulders above others in the game at that time.

He also had two great coaches in Gordon Wallace and Walter Smith and I was becoming more and more interested in the coaching side of the game.

I have personal experience of how Jim's insight both benefited the team and boosted and extended my football career at the top level.

I'd had fantastic success at Dundee United after making an exciting debut but had hit a kind of a wall in terms of my development and progress.

Let me explain, basically, my strength as a player had been as a running type of striker with pace, but one-footed, my right, and opposing defenders had cottoned on to the fact that I was a bit of a one-trick pony.

Other teams had latched on to the fact that my speed up front at that time would cause them bother, so they would play a sweeper at the back, which nullified my threat. Jim realised this, too, and told me that if I ever wanted to progress, I would need to change my game a wee bit.

I'd be about 20 years old and with around 18 months of success in the first team under my belt, but was told that unless I changed, it could be a hindrance to my playing career.

So it was decided that I would go back to the training ground for three afternoons a week with Walter and Gordon, whom I played alongside in the first team, to work on developing my left foot.

They worked tirelessly with me, getting me to shield the ball and cross with my left foot.

And in due course, that extra training, and I'm certain the coaches must have been fed up with me, worked wonders and led to the next phase of my playing career.

Sadly, I don't see that kind of commitment in players today, which is a real shame as well as a waste of talent.

As I see it, the elite echelon are in a class of their own, blessed with greater talent, and they work hard at their game to ensure they stay there. But the players just beneath that level, in my view, don't strive to join them and I just don't know why, as the rewards are so much more profitable these days.

Maybe, they realise they won't be able to join the cream in the Premier League and are just content with the level they are performing at, but it amazes me that they don't want to develop further. As the old saying goes, nothing ventured, nothing gained.

However, there are exceptions and one who readily springs to mind is Craig Noone, whom I signed in my second stint as manager of Plymouth Argyle.

I've prided myself in being able to spot the potential in players and help shape their careers.

Craig is a smashing lad and worked his socks off to become a better forward and it paid off as he went on to play in the Premier League with Cardiff City.

But I remember him coming to me at Home Park and the first question he asked in refreshing naivety was 'will I still get my wages paid in the summer?'

Nooney had been a roofer and playing non-league football in the north-west after having knock-backs earlier as he tried to become a full-time pro.

It was obvious to me that his dedication and talent set him apart, but there were others at Home Park in this period.

For example, another player I had at Plymouth who no-one had ever heard of before I signed him, is Yannick Bolasie. Yala has gone on to become a regular in the Premier League with Crystal Palace, along with another ex-Pilgrim, Jason Puncheon.

If you look at the careers of Reda Johnson and Jamie Mackie they have both prospered but one vital spark these players had in common was they worked really hard at getting better.

I believe that those boys realised they were kicking above their weight and thought themselves lucky to be given the chance. They were at the crossroads of their careers and thankfully, they've all taken the right path. It reminded me of the time when it was still a debate whether I'd leave school and become a professional footballer, or perhaps look at being part-time.

The decider for me was a summer job I took at a local laundry when my role was to take boiling-hot sheets and other equally scalding pieces of laundry out of the industrial-sized wringer and fold them correctly on the required pile.

On my feet for eight hours a day and with clothing hot enough to remove your finger-prints, that decided life and my future for me.

I was never the most academically-gifted student at school, so if I was to make my fortune it had to be through football.

Being more versatile led me to becoming the fulcrum of the side and a play-maker, in addition to becoming a consistent goalscorer.

If you remember what a great player Kenny Dalglish was, well that's who I likened myself to, even though he cost me a good many Scotland caps. The other player I greatly admired was the brilliant Jimmy Greaves, so I had world-class strikers to look up to.

Jock Stein, who was Scotland coach, recognised my frustration at the lack of opportunities because of Kenny, and although I'd not complained, he said to me if ever Dalglish wasn't able to play, I would be his automatic replacement in the Scotland team.

Nevertheless, it was galling that I was in Spain for the 1982 World Cup, but was only ever a substitute, although I played twice for Scotland in the 1986 finals in Mexico.

Basically, I watched my country in the 1982 finals as I didn't get on, although I was asked to warm up for the Brazil game, which I did at the far end of the pitch.

But when I turned around I saw that Dalglish was on the pitch, without a warm-up, so he went on and I sat down again.

But I considered myself lucky and proud to be chosen in the first place, although I was desperate to play for my country. Which I did in the next World Cup finals in 1986 by which time Fergie had replaced Jock as national coach.

Jock had died of a heart attack following Scotland's traumatic and dramatic final qualifying game against Wales at Cardiff City's Ninian Park stadium and was replaced by Fergie, who was his assistant.

Scotland had played some warm-up matches and I scored a hat-trick in one of the friendly games in Santa Fe ahead of the finals.

We played in the same group as Uruguay, Denmark and the then West Germany but managed just one point from the three matches.

During the goalless draw with Uruguay I received the by now familiar rough-house treatment of the South Americans, being pinched, elbowed and generally given a going over.

Despite the obvious disappointment of failing to get out of our group, I could at least say I'd played for my country at a World Cup finals, but I don't draw a lot of comfort from that fact.

I was to retire as a player having spent my entire footballing career with Dundee United, three years after the Mexico World Cup finals, and embarked on the rollercoaster world of management.

I could look back on a playing career, though, in which I played for only one club and scored 171 goals in 576 games.

From Player
To Manager

I WAS 32-years-old when I packed up playing, that was following the 1-0 defeat to Hamilton Academical. I walked into the dressing room and hammered six-inch nails into my boots and they stayed on the boot-room wall for three-and-a-half years.

The smell, I think, forced me to take them down, eventually.

But I'd had plenty of experience coaching and gained requisite certificates and had been the Arabs' youth, reserve-team and first-team coach at Tannadice. I then became the only coach at Dundee United with responsibility for four teams in addition to travelling down to England once a week scouting for potential signings.

I would train the youth team and when the first team came out, I would train them, too, bringing the younger, first-team players back in the afternoon, to train with the senior side.

United's youth team also played 30-odd friendlies a season against men's sides, my reasoning being that I had been toughened up by the experience at the start of my career, and was appreciative of the challenge.

It certainly worked, for Dundee United's youth team won several trophies under my watch.

Mind you when you have young guns like Duncan Ferguson and Christian Dailly in your ranks, you kind of know you're going to win more than a few matches. Big Dunc proved to be a great striker and later signed for Rangers from United for £5million and to give you an idea of what a terrific boy he was, the first thing he did after leaving us, was buy his dad a racing pigeon for £30,000. He was a pleasure to coach, too.

So, alongside my playing career, coaching was always a passion with me and so I was really flattened when I didn't get the position I wanted most – the manager's position at Dundee United.

Basically, the job was, if not promised to me, heavily hinted by Jim before he went on holiday to America, but he said the board, in his absence, had gone for the former Southampton full-back, Ivan Golac.

Naturally, I was bitterly disappointed but I stayed on as first-team coach and it soon became clear that Ivan's ideas and mine not just clashed, but were strangers to one another.

Ivan had managed at Torquay United for a while and arranged to have one of the lads he'd been on a coaching course with in England come up to Scotland, initially, to be his number two.

I had to pick the lad up, Ivan had plans for him to be assistant manager of Dundee United, but the lad himself quickly realised that it was a step too far and he would be out of his depth in the SPL.

I learned that Ivan had shared a room with him at a coaching course and the lad's link with a football club, was that he was a barman at Rochdale's social club.

To the lad's credit, he knew he wasn't to the standard, which was borne out when he was interviewed for the job and the kindest thing you can say is that it was evident to both United and the candidate that he was not what we were looking for.

It was an odd and somewhat pithy tale and the lad who had come up to Dundee on the train hoping to land a great job, left for England by the same mode of transport, without becoming Ivan's second in command.

But in a funny way that brought Ivan and myself closer together and officially I was still the assistant manager and first-team coach.

But it was an uneasy relationship and one ultimately doomed to fail.

There are plenty of examples I could relay. I remember one occasion when there was a spate of food poisoning going around the team and Ivan said that both he and I would have to play.

Now, there was no way that I was going to allow that to happen so on our way to the game, I got the players out of the team bus and into the fresh air and they improved, so our 'services' were not called upon.

Ivan had some strange ideas in training, too, and in league matches he said he wanted all the outfield players to be in the 18-yard box for corner kicks, starting with a game at Tynecastle.

But I made sure that adhering to my methods and not his were the final words the players heard before they went out on the field to face Hearts.

But the final straw came when Ivan told the board that I was not sticking to his training programme and I was called in to explain myself.

I was reprimanded by the board and told that I had to adhere to the letter of the law, although Jim McLean nearly choked on his cup of coffee when Ivan relayed the story about the corner kick and my part in getting the players to ignore it.

To be fair, the players were also panicking about Ivan's plan. With the goalie on the halfway line and everyone else in the box, it was one of those scary scenarios.

It was a disaster waiting to happen so far as I was concerned, if our opponents cleared their lines and I was dead against it and told the board so. Those were the sorts of things Ivan was advocating and I thought they were crazy.

So, there was clearly a conflict of interests going on and when St Johnstone offered me the job of manager, reluctantly, I left Dundee United.

And to rub salt into my wounds, Dundee United went on to win the Scottish Cup under Ivan's management, something big Jim and me never achieved in our time together.

But that's football for you – Ivan had inherited a quality team and he had Lady Luck not so much smiling on them as grinning from ear to ear, as on the way to Scottish Cup success as United had to win a replay in every round.

However, I was delighted for the supporters and the club celebrated United's success in winning the Scottish Cup at long last.

Leaving Tannadice for McDiarmid Park rescued me from the ridiculous situation at Dundee United and as it turned out was the making of me.

St Johnstone were in the Premier League but were something like 15 points adrift and getting relegated. That was the first time, until I took over the reins at Yeovil Town, that I was in charge of a team I had not been able to keep up.

And that was in my first job.

I honestly believe St Johnstone was a great learning curve for me and I was a more than willing student. It was a really relaxed club under the enlightened and laid-back chairmanship of Geoff Brown. For example, I recall us having board meetings on the golf course on a Friday.

In addition, he would take me away for a golf weekend at key points every year, saying 'if you're stale, you're no good to me'.

We'd go away to Portugal or Spain for four or five days' golfing and just chilling out and believe me it worked. Geoff was an innovative and sensitive chairman and better than me, saw the danger of the pressures in management even before I did.

In our promotion year with St Johnstone, I remember we were playing Airdrie in a re-arranged league game and although we were 13 points or so clear at the top of the Scottish First Division, I was still worried about losing that game or any game for that matter.

Unfortunately, the match clashed with one of our golfing trips and I had to listen to the game on the phone in a running commentary scenario.

I think we won the game 1-0 but because of the targets I'd set myself the stress levels were rising higher than is healthy.

So, Geoff's ethos of getting out of the line of fire even for a couple of days, shows he was a thoughtful chairman, conscious that I wouldn't be in the same predicament that I was before when I had taken St Johnstone to Dundee United in 1995 and suffered a stress-related attack, which ended up with me in hospital.

But it was not a heart attack as the news reports speculated at the time, although the symptoms were much the same. I had become exasperated with my side and was shouting and bawling at the players and became aware of severe pain shooting down my left arm, which ended up with me collapsing.

Luckily, there was a medical centre just behind the dug-out at Tannadice and I was treated there by the Dundee United doctor who told me he didn't think I'd had a heart attack, but would transfer me to the hospital just to make certain.

They gave me this stuff to open up the arteries, in case I'd had a heart attack, but one of the side-effects was that it gave me a shocking headache.

All I remember is having a splitting headache and was sitting alone on a trolley in the corridor, when the landline on the wall began to ring and ring and ring.

I cursed the wretched thing as there was no-one there to answer it except me and the thought of doing that and increasing the pounding in my head was not something I relished.

But in the end, I couldn't stand the ringing any longer and grabbed the phone, said 'hullo' and before I could add any other comment a voice vaguely familiar blasted at me.

'You're trying to change the mentality of players, aren't you? If they are bad trainers, get rid of them, if they've a bad attitude get rid of them, remember leopards never change their spots.'

'Who's this talking,' I said.

'It's Alex Ferguson – I've just seen the report about you on Ceefax and rang around to find out where you were.

'I hope everything is OK,' and with that he hung up.

Naturally, I was touched by his concern, not least because he was busy turning around Manchester United and was on his way to becoming the most famous manager in the country.

That's the side of Fergie you don't hear about often enough and I doubt if he told anyone about the call. I knew what Fergie had said was correct, I'd been over-stressed, over-working and got frustrated which culminated in me hyper-ventilating.

I don't think that incident contributed to the Parkinson's, it was totally unrelated, and the only after-effect, was that people kept thinking and writing that I'd had a heart attack, which was incorrect.

But I still counted myself as lucky in having the best chairman, I've ever had, Geoff Brown, and the best manager, Jim McLean. It was a brilliant coaching education all round for me.

Naturally, given the medical scare, I needed time off work away from the daily grind of life in the hot seat and, fortunately, one of the board had a holiday home in Spain, so I went there for three or four days.

I left the team in the very able hands of John Blackley, whom I took to St Johnstone with me from Dundee United. I had been impressed with John or Sloop as he's equally well known – he got the nickname from 'Sloop John B' – if you know the song.

Fortunately, I can switch off when I'm away playing golf and not trying to solve my football team's every little problem.

It's very good to unwind and I thoroughly enjoyed those breaks.

I received a real morale booster one time when I was away playing golf and it's something I'm really, really proud about.

It happened when Sean Connery was playing the same hole as us and after came into the clubhouse for a drink. Sean walked over and the first thing he said to me was: 'You're Paul Sturrock aren't you?'

Talk about a claim to fame – for a film star of Sean's world stature to say that to me and then spend 20 minutes chatting about the game with a great Scot – 007 himself – is something I'll never forget.

Nor will I ever forget the great start in football management Geoff and St Johnstone gave me.

And had it been any club but my beloved Dundee United and the chance of achieving a dream and managing my boyhood team, I probably would not have left St Johnstone.

But the St Johnstone squad when I joined them had a losing mentality and I needed to change that mindset and get them to respond to my coaching.

But that takes time, patience and pre-planning.

However, I very nearly quit as manager when after going out of the Scottish Cup to Stenhousemuir, I told the chairman I was thinking of chucking in the job.

Thankfully, and to his credit, Geoff made it abundantly clear that he wouldn't accept my resignation and gave me the green light to rebuild the team and get rid of whatever players I wanted and start all over again.

But, the bottom line was that I was going nowhere and was given the all-clear to shape the squad into my own image of what a football team should be. It took me two full seasons to get that team up and running and it ended with us winning the Division One title by a country mile and promotion back to the top flight.

I had recruited young players full of promise and desire to succeed and improve, again with the backing of the chairman.

I am very proud of my years at St Johnstone as the chairman allowed me to build a squad that won promotion into the SPL and reach a League Cup Final.

Not only that but we had a team at McDiarmid Park packed with young players who were as fit as any side in the land, and they established themselves in the Scottish top flight.

I've always held firm to the belief that if you can leave a post knowing the side you're managing is better off than when you joined them, that's a success and you can go with your head held high.

* * * * *

JOHN BLACKLEY recalls joining Paul Sturrock at the Perthshire club, which proved to be the start of a long and successful association between the two Scotland internationals. John said:

Well, Paul and me go back a wee while that's for sure.

The first time we worked together was at St Johnstone which was also his first managerial post.

That was in 1993 and Paul brought me in as assistant manager. I had been working in my home town of Falkirk, coaching in schools and so on, and thoroughly enjoying it.

Then, out of the blue, I get a call from Paul saying did I fancy coming to McDiarmid Park? And Paul being Paul added by the way you weren't my first choice, I've asked a couple of other guys before you. I thought well, that's nice to know.

Anyway, it wasn't a problem and I went up to see him in Perth and thought it was great.

We didn't know each other that well, prior to that, we had played against each other a couple of times, but there wasn't much history between us. But it was a great start for me and we went on to have an extremely successful period together which took in Dundee United, Plymouth twice, Sheffield Wednesday and Swindon.

It was great just to be part of it at St Johnstone and also in England. Naturally enough Paul's the main man and it has been great to be part of that journey.

When I joined Paul at St Johnstone the team were already struggling and were relegated in that first season, but we took it to the very end of the campaign.

But to be fair to the chairman, Geoff Brown, he never changed his mind or his views on what he wanted for St Johnstone and he stuck with Paul. That was a great time for me and we built a really good side with some really good youngsters coming through the ranks and we also bought one or two players to strengthen that unit.

During the remainder of our time at St Johnstone, we won promotion from Division One to the Scottish Premier League and I felt we left them in a very strong position.

St Johnstone finished third in the league and got through to cup quarter-finals and semi-finals – they were a very fine side and from my point of view it was a great pleasure to coach these boys.

The thing with Paul is that he had a picture of the future and if you don't have that then you won't build a successful team, that is key.

Paul's picture involved bringing in the right players and coaching them correctly and to be fair, the chairman was always willing to help with money for signings, particularly with up-and-coming footballers.

So, it works both ways, with management and chairman singing off the same hymn sheet and at St Johnstone, that was most certainly the case.

✽ ✽ ✽ ✽ ✽

FROM PLAYER TO MANAGER

GEOFF BROWN remembers:

There had been a debate about bringing in Paul for his first real managerial position, but such was the esteem in which he was held as a coach and although we had others in the frame, he was by far the best candidate.

Like he is at Yeovil Town, Paul joined our club when we were already sunk and so it was no reflection on him that his first proper season as manager was in Division One.

He set about strengthening and bringing in players he felt best suited the style of football he was to demand from the team.

It took the next season for the team to settle into a shape that Paul was reasonably satisfied with and later to be very happy with, as much as a manager like Paul can be.

The players responded to his demands and thought the world of him and he brought the club success which we'd never had before.

It was a real wrench for Paul to leave us and if it hadn't been the pull of managing Dundee United under his own steam, I don't think he would have done.

Dundee United were underperforming and due to Paul's long association with them, you could tell he felt he had to do something about their plight.

But I maintain that if Paul hadn't left St Johnstone when he did, then he would have been a candidate for the Scotland coach's position.

He was a young first-team coach who had brought with him fresh ideas and a work ethic he had soaked up in his time at Tannadice under Jim McLean.

On a personal level, Paul and me became firm friends and we had a trust between manager and chairman that I hadn't experienced before or since then.

I recall one day he said 'listen come down to England with me, I want your opinion on a player that I've been told about'.

The game was at Molineux where Wolves were playing Manchester United and the player he'd been alerted to was playing for the home side.

At half-time I said of the potential target that he didn't look any better than what we had in the St Johnstone first team, but there was one player in the United side who looked a very good prospect.

Paul agreed and said he would sound out Alex Ferguson in the morning. True to his word, Paul duly called Fergie, who must have had a sixth sense about the purpose of Luggy's query and cut him short saying: 'Fuck off Sturrock, he's not for sale.' The player in question was a very youthful Paul Scholes and Luggy has since praised me for being an astute judge of talent.

FROM PLAYER TO MANAGER

* * * * *

EAMONN BANNON on Paul Sturrock – the former Scotland, Hearts, Chelsea and Dundee United midfielder shares his experiences of playing with Sturrock. Bannon's £165,000 transfer fee in 1979 from Chelsea to Tannadice was then a Scottish record.

I joined Dundee United in 1979 and left in 1988 so I had the best part of 10 years with Paul.

When I arrived at the club Paul was already there and when I left Tannadice he was still there so he went on to play for another three years, as a coach and later on manage them, so he had a long association with Dundee United.

After I left Dundee United, I went to Hearts in Edinburgh and when Paul became manager of St Johnstone, he wanted me to go and join him but I was already a reserve team coach at Hibernian and so that just couldn't work out. The money St Johnstone were offering was poorer, too. It's one of those crossroads-in-life moments when you look back and wonder what would have happened if I'd made a different decision.

I think of all the Dundee United players that I played with and we were all really close pals, Paul is easily the one who has had the most successful managerial career.

I think what sets Paul apart and what he has that other managers didn't have is a kind of quirkiness, he believed in doing things a little bit differently.

For example, at St Johnstone, he took the players canoeing and mountain climbing, a wee bit off-the-wall sort of stuff but at the same time he had a very well disciplined team and they were definitely well coached.

From an early age, leastways in football terms, Paul was very much into his coaching and he would go off to Canada for a couple of weeks in the close season.

I had a young family and the last thing I wanted to do was to go off to Canada and coach at a summer camp, but that's what Paul did.

There's no doubt that Jim McLean was a terrific coach and Paul would have learned from him during his long playing career at Dundee United, however, I've never actually seen Paul coach. But as a manager you're judged on how successful you are and Paul has been very successful at certain clubs.

We were a very close unit at Dundee United and all the guys in that period were always interested in how Paul is getting on as a manager, at St Johnstone, Sheffield Wednesday, Plymouth and with Southampton in the Premier League.

It's not very often a Scottish player, who had basically spent all his life in Scotland, goes down and does well in the English league. Alex Ferguson springs to mind, obviously, Gordon Strachan had a stab at one or two, but Paul has clearly achieved that. At St Johnstone Paul's team played good football and he brought about success on a shoestring budget.

The one thing that struck me about watching Paul's St Johnstone was that they played exactly the same way that we did at Dundee United, a very strong 4-4-2 formation, everyone knew their position and there was no messing about, and that was Jim McLean's trademark.

* * * * *

Acclaimed centre-back JIM WEIR, now manager of Elgin, also has great memories from his time under Paul Sturrock at McDiarmid Park – and some painful ones, too. He said:

I had played in Paul's last game as a player for Dundee United – I was playing for Hamilton Accies and we beat them 1-0 and I think that must have been enough for him.

He hung up his boots after that game. Paul signed me as a player from Hearts in November 1994, I think it was. He brought me in as a centre-back for St Johnstone, Paul's first club as a manager in his own right.

I stayed on for 13 years and got to see Paul's coaching at first hand.

Paul gave me the captaincy quite soon after joining and I went on to play over 200 games for Saints before injury curtailed my playing career and I eventually went into management.

I was unlucky with injuries and had 22 operations including fixing a broken jaw and busted nose. I remember breaking my nose really badly against Dundee and it was so bad that after the game when Paul saw how horrific it was he almost passed out, as did a few of the other guys.

But although I may not have been the most gifted of footballers, Paul liked me for my commitment and toughness and said I would always be one of the first names on his team sheet.

His trust in me was repaid as I believe a captain leads from the front and despite the serious nose injury, I played in St Johnsone's next three games.

Paul already had a great working relationship with John Blackley off the pitch and I was able to influence matters on the park.

Both Paul and Sloop were very, very thorough in everything they did.

Paul is easily the best coach that I have ever worked with – his dedication and attention to detail and getting the lowdown on other teams is second to none.

He knew every player and would sit up and watch games into the early hours of the morning – he was meticulous in his preparation.

I was not surprised that Paul did so well in his first job in England with Plymouth Argyle, after all he'd won a championship with St Johnstone up here in Scotland.

When he returned to Dundee United, the team that he left at St Johnstone went on to finish third in the league that season. I was absolutely gutted when he left McDiarmid Park but was delighted that he was given the opportunity to manage a team like Dundee United.

I know that he already followed the game in England and so I wasn't at all surprised that he was able to adapt and gain success down south with Argyle.

Paul knew how to get results from his teams and that was due in no small measure to his attention to detail on the opposition.

I went down to watch Paul's League One play-off semi-finals when he was at Sheffield Wednesday and was utterly amazed at the support at that club which went on to win the promotion.

Personally, I've taken an awful lot of my experience of playing under Paul into my managerial career – I've managed four clubs, including where I am now at Elgin. I knew Paul's reputation but did not find him daunting as person, although he was always challenging me to keep my first-team place which kept me on my toes.

He placed a big emphasis on fitness and competition for places and in training brought an intensity to the job and put demands on his players.

One of Paul's famous statements was 'train as you play' meaning if you are sloppy in training then you'll be sloppy in games.

As player, Paul was an outstanding striker and had a terrific balance about him as well as being tremendously fit. Even though he had a small frame he was remarkably robust and versatile and that is something he has drummed into his players as a manager – the importance of link-up play with your fellow forwards.

And that is something that has stuck with me and work at constantly, the importance of movement.

I speak to Paul pretty much every day and he is genuinely interested in how I am doing and keen to praise.

He is generous with his time and advice, which has continued from when I was a player under him at St Johnstone. I believe he felt I was someone who could handle criticism and although he can come across as bluff, I found him succinct and to the point.

Paul played under Jim McLean's management style at Dundee United, and was clearly influenced by Jim, but evolved into his own man.

I honestly thought he was certainly a good enough coach to manage an international side.

I know he has been offered a number of jobs in Scotland but he loves it down in the south west and is very happy where he is.

One of the funnies I remember from his time at St Johnstone came when Paul was railing against one of our players, Roddy Grant, during the half-time break and looked set to throw a cup, which was full of tea, at the player.

However, Roddy was afraid of no-one and Roddy shot him such a fierce look that Paul was so unnerved that he ended up nearly throwing the tea all over himself.

The St Johnstone team he managed had a team spirit that was unrivalled I believe and thanks to Paul and John Blackley.

Every player will have nothing but praise for the pair of them, as they were improved as players by the experience.

They were ahead of their time in terms of going to great lengths to watch games and become knowledgeable on players from African countries like Algeria.

LUGGY

*Before the number of TV stations we have now —
Paul somehow got himself a huge satellite dish so he could
analyse teams overseas.*

*There wasn't a player you could mention that Paul
and John didn't already have a good knowledge about.*

Back At
Dundee United

I AGONISED over whether to return to Dundee United as the team I had assembled at St Johnstone was youthful, hungry, fit and successful.

But having failed to land the Dundee United job the first time, it was like an itch I couldn't scratch and I knew I couldn't turn it down once it came up again.

After about six months back at Tannadice, I told the board of my plan to revamp the squad and bring in young players, as the side at that time was sterile in my opinion and packed with overseas players who couldn't or wouldn't respond to my coaching demands. It was a struggle at first but many of the players I brought in went on to bigger and better things.

Billy Dodds was the catalyst for everything that was good at Dundee United and whenever he played we won.

I'd had Billy at St Johnstone, signing him for a club record fee of £400,000 in January 1994 from Dundee for whom he had been a prolific striker, before he left for Aberdeen where he was also extremely successful.

I signed him from the Dons for £700,000 as part of a deal that saw Robbie Winters go to Pittodrie in September 1998.

Billy was an instant success at Tannadice and scored a hat-trick on his debut against St Johnstone and thus became a hero figure for the Arabs' fans.

As I said Billy was an integral player for us at United and was key to our rebuilding process at Tannadice.

Then Rangers came into the picture and decided they wanted to take Billy and I was adamant that he must stay with Dundee United.

But Billy said that he wanted to move to Rangers and in a tearful conversation, he said that I was standing in his way.

So I had to give in and Billy moved 15 months after I'd signed him for £1.3million to Rangers who at that time were managed by Dick Advocaat.

I had bought and sold him twice over, but it was with regret Dundee United allowed Billy to leave for Rangers.

But if you look at the figures, I'd bought him for around £400,000 from Dundee, sold him for £600,000 from Aberdeen in a swap deal – so basically, Billy had joined us for free.

Robbie was an up and coming striker, but I didn't fancy him, whereas I had lots of time for Billy so the swap deal suited me.

The transfer itself is a great story and worth relating.

Alex Miller, the Aberdeen manager, out of the blue came on the phone and said 'I'd like to buy Robbie Winters', so I then said, 'What's the story with Doddsy, do you fancy a swap?'

He said: 'How much would you want for Winters', and I said to John Blackley my assistant manager, 'he's offering money as well' bearing in mind Dodds was a Scottish international.

Miller said: 'How about £200,000, would that be acceptable?' and I put my hand over the phone and said he's offering £200k as well as Doddsy.

I stalled and said, 'No, that would nae do it, I've a board to convince, as Winters is an up-and-coming star, whereas Doddsy would do me in the short term.'

Miller replied: 'Well, what about £400,000?'

Again I put my hand over the phone and told Sloop, and thought I'll push my luck a bit here and told Alex after a bit more quick-thinking and nifty footwork, 'If you give me £500,000 plus another £100,000 for Robbie if he wins an international call.'

So, the deal was done and in all I got £600,000 when I sold him to Aberdeen, another £600,000 when I bought him back from Aberdeen, and £1.3million from Rangers, a rolling figure of around £2.2million.

It made financial sense, but we paid a price on the pitch, as Dundee United won just two games for the rest of the season and from being in the top three when Doddsy was with us, we finished eighth at the end of the season.

I was coming under pressure from the board at United to go down the transfer route, buying overseas players, rather than allow the young squad I was building to mature and for the side to reap the rewards that I knew they would deliver.

So, once again, I was at odds with the board at Tannadice over policy and was left with no option but to quit a couple of games in to the 2000/01 season.

That was my last stint as a manager in Scotland and my next job was about as far away from Dundee as it was to possible to get.

* * * * *

Former Scotland international defender, JOHN BLACKLEY, who moved from St Johnstone with Sturrock, had a foreboding over his partner's return to Tannadice. He said:

I didn't fancy Paul going to Dundee United as I felt it was the wrong move and he was doing it for the wrong if admirable reason.

I'd made a similar move myself, when I went back to manage Hibernian and wanted them to be as successful as when I'd played for them.

I knew Paul wanted to run Dundee United in the same fashion as when Jim McLean had managed them. But it needs time, a little bit of luck, and encouragement for him from above, so I always felt it was going to be difficult for him. But we went, and Paul wanted to go back and build up Dundee United into what it was, with Paul as manager and me as his assistant.

LUGGY

We were about two-and-half-years into the job and things weren't going that well for us and I knew Paul had had enough.

Funnily enough, we were playing Hibs and Paul, unusually, didn't travel on the team bus and we met up at this wee pub and we had a talk and he says: 'I don't think it's working out.'

I said I thought he was wrong, but it was clear he was under a lot of pressure, trying to get success while living in Dundee added to the stress and obviously also didn't help.

Paul packed the job in on the Monday after speaking to the chairman and giving him the reasons why he wanted to leave.

So, that was it for Paul at Dundee United, and a nice guy called Alex Smith came into the job and he asked me to stay on as his assistant. I had a year and a half still on my contract, so I stayed on.

Anyway then Paul had the opportunity to go to Plymouth of all places. I didn't know much about Plymouth or the south-west, let alone just how far away it was from anywhere.

But the rest is history from that point of view.

Plymouth Argyle – South Of The Border Down Devonshire Way

I HAD long harboured an ambition to manage in England and so with me severing links with my beloved Dundee United at the start of the 2000/01 season, there was no reason for me to stay in Scotland. I was out of work for the first time in my life and didn't really know what the future held for me, except that I would need to find employment.

It was David 'Budgie' Byrne who tipped me off about the managerial vacancy at Plymouth Argyle, who were stuck near the basement of the English Football League's lowest division.

I didn't know Budgie really at all in those days, our paths had crossed while I was a manager at St Johnstone and he was a player. He'd had some other football clubs up in Scotland, although, to be fair, I didn't know him from Adam, but he knew I'd left Dundee United and was out of work.

Budgie, who had played for Argyle in the late 80s and early 90s, already had a job as a football coach down at the local Plymouth College of Further Education, and reckoned it was just the challenge I needed.

I reckoned differently, believing that the Argyle board would be put off by my supposed wage demands.

But I applied anyway, although convinced I'd no chance of getting the job, Budgie whom I said I really didn't know from Adam, said you're out of work, what have you got to lose?

Despite my reservations I took Budgie's advice and applied for the post of Plymouth Argyle manager, with bag packed and an open mind over what the future held for me.

I stayed overnight at a bed and breakfast just outside of Tiverton, which was as far away from where I had spent my entire football career up to that date.

I was interviewed at Tiverton but had the feeling that the Argyle chairman, Dan McCauley, had a preference for one of the other candidates.

But the rest of the board felt differently. Nevertheless, I returned to Scotland and awaited the outcome, not with the greatest feeling of confidence. In point of fact, my interview at Plymouth was the first in my career as I'd been head-hunted for the St Johnstone post and also offered the position with Dundee United, so this was a new experience for me.

Anyway, a few days later I got a call from Paul Stapleton, who was on the board and later to become chairman of Argyle and a close friend, saying: 'Would you accept this amount of money?'

I said yes and so the deal was agreed over the phone and I flew down to the south-west without having so much as seen the city let alone the football ground.

Dan picked me up from Bristol airport and the difference between the Argyle owner/chairman and probably the best chairman I'd ever worked with, Geoff Brown at St Johnstone, was the sun and the moon.

I don't think you could dislike Dan but he was eccentric to say the least and totally unpredictable. Jim McLean up at Dundee United was a great manager, as I've said earlier and will continue to maintain, right up there with Fergie. But Jim was a novice as a chairman as I found out at Tannadice.

But nothing prepared me for the experience of working with Dan McCauley and the journey back from Bristol to Plymouth gave me an insight into his character.

He admitted that I wasn't his first choice but was overruled by the other members of the Argyle board, which was unsettling for someone like me, totally out of his comfort zone.

During the trip down to Plymouth Dan actually burst into tears, so passionate was he about Plymouth Argyle Football Club, but his outpouring of emotion more than a trifle disconcerting for a hard-nosed Scot like me.

Dan said that one of the managers he had given money to had failed and so the next manager, Kevin Hodges, he admitted that he hadn't given him any money at all – and he had also failed to deliver success for Argyle. His plea to me was, 'I don't care what it takes and what you have to do, just please keep us in the Football League.'

Argyle had lost six of their first 10 league games that season and were bumping along the bottom of the third division, so the first thing on my agenda was to halt the slide. But it was going to take a lot of work and thought.

And when I did see Home Park, to say I was unimpressed was a massive understatement.

The club was in disarray from the top to the bottom, nobody so far as I could establish had any job spec, and it showed with the officials coming in when they felt like it and basically, being out of their depth.

For example, the club secretary, a young girl, was off with stress, while the chief executive had no real experience of football at all.

The chain of command was such that if you wanted so much as a pencil, you had to send off a chitty to Rotolok, the chairman's company. The trouble was even if I was inclined to do so, which I definitely wasn't, there was no-one to pass the request on to.

The commercial department was also a shambles and not making the most of what the club had to offer. I found out that the car park next to the ground wasn't charging for parking and swiftly put an end to that situation.

LUGGY

People complained about having to pay but I pointed out that they'd had over six years of free parking, to which they had no justifiable answer.

But that was later on and as nothing to my complete shock of my first view of Home Park.

When I first saw the ground I couldn't believe it. The condition of the pitch and the training facility was terrible, due to the heavy rain that had fallen and continued to fall.

I'm from Scotland where we're not unfamiliar with rain, but I'd never experienced anything like the conditions underfoot at Plymouth.

And this would have only been in the autumn. So, in short, my first impression of Plymouth Argyle FC was that the state of the facilities at Home Park accurately resembled the club's league position, near the bottom of English football's bottom tier.

Basically, the pitch resembled a bog and to add to the surreal arrangements, there was a cherry-picker outside the main gates to accommodate the local media whom Dan had banned from reporting from the press box inside Home Park.

So, there I was many, many miles from where I grew up and was well known and at a football club that was, if not bottom of the league, then perilously close to it.

Because of the wet weather, we couldn't stage any games nor could we get in any training sessions, because Harper's Field resembled a swamp.

The problem with the Home Park pitch was my first serious concern and I had to move fast to try and get it fit for use. There was a big hole in the pitch, so large you could have fallen into it, which is where the ground staff had been trying to unblock the drains and which was doing no good at all.

Before that they had over-rolled the pitch which meant that surface water was squeezed further into the already saturated subsoil.

In the end we had to literally drill holes into the ground and with the use of small explosions – I kid you not – the water could reach the drains and run off effectively.

The next obstacle to the pitch repair was that all the soil and turf that had been dug up had been taken away and disposed of, which I found intensely irritating. Therefore the only other option left to me was to dig up the turf at Harper's Park training ground and back fill into Home Park, so we could at least stage games.

Talk about all hands to the proverbial pump, well in point of fact, mine as I decided to run the place myself.

LUGGY

I helped on the commercial side of things, revamping the club shop, which had water pouring in through the roof, which ruined the merchandise like shirts and kits. Added to which, we were into a football season and I had a squad of players who were simply not good enough, so it was an inauspicious beginning to life in English management.

More than once, I asked myself whether I had done the right thing in moving to Plymouth, but my commitment to Plymouth and to succeeding in management in England was strong.

I hadn't moved from family down from Scotland and was living alone in a flat owned by one of the board in the Beacon Park area of the city.

* * * * *

DAVID BYRNE'S thoughts on Sturrock at Plymouth and his part in not only suggesting him for the post but also acting as an intermediary between the Argyle board and the candidate:

I knew Paul Sturrock from my time playing in Scotland and I also knew that Argyle were looking for a new manager after the sacking of Hodgy (Kevin Hodges) just a few games into the season.

It was perfect timing as Paul had left Dundee United and was out of work and so I suggested he get in touch with the board down at Plymouth.

I had no qualms about Paul's ability as a coach and manager having witnessed what he achieved at St Johnstone and also his experience as a player and coach at Dundee United.

I reckoned that he would weave his magic at Home Park, bringing the same intensity and dedication that he'd shown in Scotland down to the West Country.

Paul had his interview but the only stumbling block was the salary he'd been on at Dundee United and St Johnstone which was more than Plymouth would be able to afford.

So, I asked Paul (Sturrock) what his last wage was and then asked Paul Stapleton, then a director at Plymouth, what they would be willing to pay.

I told Paul what Argyle's offer was and he accepted and the two parties were brought together.

And the rest, as they say, is history.

Breathing New Life Into The Jaded Pilgrims

MY FIRST game in charge was against Torquay United and I let the coaching staff look after the squad while I watched from the directors' box which was behind the goal.

We drew 1-1 but that point wasn't enough to keep Argyle from being either bottom or second bottom of the basement division in the English Football League.

I'd inherited quite a decent-sized squad, the trouble was that not many of them were very good. I ran the rule over them in training and none of them looked very caring about playing for Argyle, there was that kind of malaise in the camp.

There were people playing out of position and fitness levels were poor and I'm not being derogatory of my predecessor as I think it was all he could do, to be hands-on.

So, it was obvious that I needed to strengthen the squad and I was so frustrated at getting knocked back in my efforts to bring in new signings that I decided to take matters into my own hands and I signed two players without clearance from the board.

I had to browbeat the young club secretary into signing the papers, taking full responsibility for the actions myself.

I didn't know what the board would think about my actions and I was less than confident what Dan McCauley would say, but I'd already made my own mind up that I would resign at the next board meeting anyway.

The board meeting was unbelievable with the accountant who was handling the financial side of the club, shouting and bawling claiming it was not my place to by-pass the board, blah, blah, blah.

All the other board members were very quiet waiting on what Dan was going to say or what action he would take, as was I.

Unbelievably, Dan backed my actions, saying I'd done the right thing and that the squad needed new players adding that if I wasn't able to do my job, there was no point in having a manager.

It was a shock to everybody and it gave me the confidence to carry on making the changes I knew were badly needed if Argyle were to improve.

Around this period of rebuilding Dan decided he had had enough of being chairman having waited until the new stands had been built.

So, it was all change at the top with Peter Jones and Michael Foot joining the board and Paul Stapleton taking over as chairman.

I believe Dan had had enough and didn't fancy another relegation campaign, so there was a wind of change blowing into the Pilgrims' sails.

The new board revamped Argyle's affairs off the pitch and were mindful of the changes I wanted on the playing side. My first two signings were Brian McGlinchey and David Worrell. Brian came on a free from Gillingham and David had been with me at Dundee United. Both were defenders, David moving to Plymouth on loan before signing permanently and staying with Argyle for four years.

I also had two French players on trial who were to go on and have great careers with Argyle – David

Friio and Romain Larrieu. I had signed both as trialists, and included Friio, plus Brian and David, in the line-up for our first game away at Exeter City. We won 2-0 which was terrific seeing as they were our nearest league rivals and Argyle had not won away for something like two years.

The coach driver said well done to me as Argyle hadn't beaten Exeter for a number of years, so I said thanks for that and just as I said it a brick smashed into the window close to where I was sitting.

It was as if to remind me of the rivalry between the two Devon clubs. Exeter were in the bottom two or three as well as Torquay United, who were also struggling in the 2000/01 season.

That result coupled with a 1-0 victory at home to York City helped turn the tide at Plymouth, who had started poorly with one point from their opening three matches.

I was starting to put together my own team, letting players go, while keeping and improving young footballers at the club like Paul Wotton, who went on to have a glorious career at his home-town club and deciding which players I was going to retain at the end of that inaugural season.

I brought in striker Mickey Evans from Bristol Rovers who was the best signing I made in my first spell at Plymouth, and centre-back Graham Coughlan from Livingston, plus versatile defender and midfielder Lee Hodges who had been with Reading.

Coughlan and Wotton went on to be my central defenders and with Romain in goal and Mickey up front, we had a solid spine to the team. We had a nice nucleus of footballers who would play in the positions I asked them to and learn their trade.

What impressed me about Wottsie is that he is a fast learner as the advice I gave him about not letting a forward get on the wrong side of him, stuck.

That and his ability stood him in good stead for the remainder of his football career.

But Mickey's influence on the field in leading from the front and in the dressing room was immense, and I cannot speak highly enough of his efforts on behalf of Plymouth Argyle.

I brought in Jason Bent from Canada, who I spotted when I had been on a coaching course, and he proved to be extremely successful in midfield.

Friio had come to Argyle as a centre-half or defensive midfield player but after watching him score with a great header in a training session, I reasoned he'd be effective in a more attacking role.

David was dubious at first but took to the role and became a most feared and effective box-to-box goalscoring and attacking midfielder. So my hunch paid off and David, who had joined us with his career seemingly going nowhere playing in the second or third division in France, never looked back and eventually went on to play Championship football with Nottingham Forest.

Both Romain and David were super ambassadors for the club, on and off the pitch.

The squad was starting to take shape and the picture of the squad I wanted I had in my mind's eye when I first took over, was nearing fruition.

So, from an inauspicious start in my first season in charge, Argyle finished well clear of the relegation zone in 12th place and ready for a push on in the next season, 2001/02.

I put together a new back four plus an effective unit in midfield where young players like Stevie Adams forced his way into the first team seemingly having come from nowhere. I'd had no comprehension of Stevie who was in the youth team when I joined the club, but he became an important player for me, as did Kevin Wills and Buster Phillips.

There was no looking back and the confidence started to flow and I knew, especially in our promotion season, that if we scored first, then you'd bet on us to win home or away.

And remember, when I came to Plymouth, they'd not won an away game for two years, something ridiculous like that. It was key for me that the team must be prepared properly for away matches.

I must admit, though, that when I first moved to Plymouth I really struggled with the travelling. You have to remember that in Scotland, at the most, it's a two-hour journey, which I thought was a long time, that is until you manage in Plymouth.

Getting to Bristol took two hours from Plymouth, so it was a struggle, given that we had to play at places like Hartlepool and Carlisle.

Therefore, we decided that we'd have to make away trips more pleasurable and in the end, particularly in the promotion season, it was much more relaxed, even though on a couple of occasions, funny things happened that weren't pre-planned.

On one of our away trips, at Lincoln, I remember the coach driver got us lost in the city, which took some doing given you could see the ground from our hotel.

But he took us, don't ask me why, in the complete opposite direction, believing he knew a quicker route. It wasn't and we were almost late for the actual match.

Another time at Shrewsbury after a pre-match meal, we came back to the changing room to find, to our horror and anger, some idiot or idiots, presumably linked with the hosts, had soaked the players' boots which were in a container and which couldn't be dried out in time.

This meant the squad had to play in squelchy and uncomfortable attire. If I remember rightly Shrewsbury beat us that day.

A lot has been said and written about the period and how closely-knit the players were and how that was important to our success. They did and it wasn't a phony thing, either, as the players' girlfriends and wives got on socially, which in turn helped to form a stronger bond for the lads.

I found it crucial that when you sign for a geographically remote employer, compared to most league football clubs, that you live in the city and get to know your surroundings and colleagues better.

There were a lot of genuine friendships forged in that period, as well as a lot of hard work on the training ground, both in the mornings and afternoons. And no friendship was closer at that time than mine with the chairman, Paul Stapleton, which is why it is such a shame that our relationship ended in my second spell in charge of Argyle.

But all through my time at Plymouth I got on well with the supporters and went to a few of the meet the manager nights. I've always felt that supporters, whichever club I've been at, are appreciative of honesty and openness and at Plymouth that was certainly the case.

I know and understand the exasperation of fans, especially if they feel they don't know what their football club is up to, and I hope I've been respected for refusing to shy away from question and answer sessions.

In the early days and onwards at Plymouth, after training sessions, I'd sit in the wee office inside the ground, willing to listen to the views of the Green Army, usually accompanied by a pot of tea.

The Far Post club at Home Park was a fantastic place and I'd make a point of after-match discussions with the supporters, win, lose or draw, who would let me know their woes and what they thought was wrong with the football club.

That was a fantastic time for me and Argyle and the Green Army. You could feel something special was brewing at Home Park, crowds were flocking back to watch us home and away.

John Blackley, known to everyone as Sloop, came down from Dundee United to join me at Plymouth for my second season, which turned out to be our promotion year – 2001/02.

Sloop initially came down for a month to play golf and I persuaded him to become defensive coach, after getting clearance from the board, joining me and forwards' coach Kevin Summerfield on the coaching staff.

Over the next couple of years, I brought in players who I felt would move us on like Hasney Aljofree, Nathan Lowndes and Marino Keith, along with Peter Gilbert and Tony Capaldi, giving Argyle more flexibility and solidity.

A defender, Hasney, had been with me at Dundee United and he joined us in 2002, as did Nathan, whom I had signed for St Johnstone, while fellow striker Marino, a Peterhead boy, came to Home Park in November 2001.

Both Peter and Tony I added to the squad in 2003 on free transfers from Birmingham City, and they, too, went on to have big careers with Plymouth.

Another player whom I signed, initially on loan from Bolton Wanderers, was David 'Chuck' Norris, in autumn 2002 and he was to play over 200 times for Argyle in the next six years and become a very important figure in the club's rise up the divisions.

Our goals against ratio was very impressive and I knew that if we scored first then we were solid enough to either win or draw the game.

That was down to hard work on the training ground. So from looking down and out in 2000, Argyle were promoted as 2001/02 champions from what was then Division Three with a total of 102 points a season later. We'd scored 71 times and conceded just 28 goals giving us a goal-difference record of +43.

The lads had promotion guaranteed before the end of March and with a 3-1 victory away to Rochdale, it was a fantastic feeling at Spotland knowing whatever happened we'd be playing in the division above the next season.

Our confidence was sky high and we were determined to finish the season in style by winning the title which we did, thus spiking the guns of our rivals for top spot, Luton Town.

Ain't no stopping us now seemed to be the theme running through the dressing room and the momentum we had gathered was irresistible. We celebrated going up as league champions with an emphatic 4-1 victory at Darlington in our penultimate match of the campaign at Feethams on April 15.

Already assured of promotion on March 26, Argyle enjoyed their triumphant tour of the north-east by beating Carlisle United 2-0, also away, three days earlier.

The Darlington game stands out for a very personal reason as my mum, who is based in the north-east, came down to watch her son's Plymouth Argyle win their first championship since 1959.

Over 18,000 fans watched our final match of the season at Home Park against Cheltenham which we also won, 2-0.

At Carlisle, it was decided we would wear our next season's change strip of tangerine shirts and white shorts for the first time, the only trouble being that the shorts were far too big and the closer it got to kick-off the more people were panicking.

So, we had to wear our green shorts instead, which later became our kit of choice.

But the funny thing was that one of the staff said 'look, look, the fans must have already been aware of the shirts because there's loads of them wearing tangerine shirts on the terraces'.

So, I looked and sure enough there was around 150–200 spectators with tangerine shirts, but they weren't members of the Green Army but Dundee United supporters come down to see my team celebrate in style. It was a very moving moment for me and these boys would come to the nearest point geographically to Dundee to support one of my teams.

The following season was one of consolidation in what is now League One and then the second division and we finished respectably just outside the play-offs, more than holding our own.

The 2003/04 season brought us our second promotion in two years, but by the time the champagne was on ice, I had left to become manager of Southampton, leaving Argyle in the capable hands of caretaker manager, Summers and new boss Bobby Williamson.

* * * * *

For someone who would go on to forge one of the most successful manager/assistant manager partnerships in the Football League for the next decade, KEVIN SUMMERFIELD admitted he knew little or nothing about Paul Sturrock until the Scot was appointed in 2000.

No, I hadn't really heard about Luggy so it was a whole new experience working together for both of us.

I had only been coaching for about four years and had been in charge of the youth team at Plymouth, so the name Paul Sturrock didn't ring any bells.

I had been working as caretaker manager of the first team for the opening few games of the 2000/01 League Two season after Kevin Hodges was sacked and recognised that I enjoyed looking after the senior side and couldn't see myself being involved in the youth side out of choice.

Anyway, that decision was made for me when Paul was named as the new Argyle boss. I met him and we sat down and had a chat and Paul said I'm going to give you an opportunity to assist me and if you prove yourself, then you'll have a good chance of getting the job.

Which is how it turned out as in 2000/01 it was important to stabilise the league position.

Sloop came down to join us from Dundee United the following season as defence coach and, well, you know the rest.

What is the secret to Luggy's success?

Well, he has a formidable knowledge of football and what he doesn't know he learns very quickly, particularly when I first met him about the lower divisions of the Football League and how they operate.

He knew exactly what he wanted us to do and how he wanted his team to play, so it was a really clear vision for him and as long as the side stuck to that, it was pretty easy.

I worked on the forwards, Sloop on the defenders, and Luggy would sit on the side and watch and if anything needed to be said, he would.

But to be fair, he let his coaches get on with it, so obviously he was happy with what we were providing.

Yes, we did work very, very hard on fitness and the running sessions Paul brought down to England with him, that he learned in Scotland.

I still use them now at Birmingham City and we have a couple of Scottish players on the books, and they knew straight away that they were brought down from Scotland. Another thing with Paul's managerial style is that he very rarely lost his temper, whether at Southampton, Sheffield, Swindon or wherever.

One of Paul's strengths is that perhaps with the exception of Southampton, he likes to involve everybody in the club, whether they are cleaners, coaches or players.

That produced a relaxed and positive atmosphere where you actually enjoy going to work and have a bit of a laugh, which leads to a strong spirit of unity at pretty much every club he's worked at. Paul had that gift in spades.

When Paul left Plymouth to join Southampton, I was caretaker again at the end of the 2003/04 League One season at the conclusion of which Argyle went up as champions.

It was a happy and successful time and a learning curve at Plymouth first time around and I was delighted to join Paul as his assistant at Southampton in the Premier League.

* * * * *

PAUL STAPLETON, former Argyle chairman remembers the start of the 'wonderful journey together' with Paul Sturrock.

He said:

After joining the board in June 1998 and having experienced a manager being sacked within five minutes of me sitting at the table I had only experienced Kevin Hodges as manager. Kevin had had a really hard job working under Dan McCauley. I helped him as much as I could but both our hands were tied.

However two years later we were looking for a new manager with Dan looking for a change.

Appointments were made for a Sunday at Rotolok offices and managers came for interview.

I realised that Dan had a favourite in Ian Atkins as when he left Dan said put the champagne on ice.

We had interviewed four people with two more to follow later including Kevin Summerfield. Dan had discussed with us the likely salary but not to candidates.

I liked Paul Sturrock who was engaging, knowledgable and who had a twinkle in his eye. However when asked about money he gave the impression he was used to double or treble what we were prepared to offer.

When they had left Dan asked for a straw poll. Only John McNulty voted for Paul, although I did make it clear this vote wasn't binding.

I took it that Paul was out of our reach, financially.

On the following Saturday before our Kidderminster game I was doorstepped by David Byrne who asked me what I thought of Paul. I said I liked him but he was out of our price range. David asked me how much and then to my surprise said Paul would come for that. I was amazed but delighted.

The game was called off so we took the opportunity to interview Kevin and then look to appoint a new manager.

After three hours Ann McCauley said to Dan that we should come to a decision as it was time to go home.

Dan wanted Ian Atkins, Peter Bloom didn't mind, Ken Jones wanted Kevin and I wanted Paul. Dan owned *the club so he could have who he wanted but I did say to him not to say the decision for his choice was unanimous as it wouldn't be. We discussed pros and cons of all candidates. I had Ian Atkins' most recent stats and they were poor. I kept coming back to the new broom from Scotland.*

Eventually and to my surprise Dan said ok, go with Paul. He asked me to ring Paul Sturrock the next day to do the deal. Well done David Byrne, you changed history.

I rang Paul who was pleased to hear the news, saying he was about to go to Cyprus and would come down the next day to Plymouth.

I was asked to take Paul out to the Copthorne Hotel for a meal. We got on very well from the start.

The following May, Dan asked me and Peter Jones to put together a consortium to buy him out. We managed this somehow and on the day before the next season we took control. Paul wasn't happy at first. I think he liked Dan deep down, indeed I had always got on with him and can appreciate all he did for the club.

Soon after Paul embraced us and was like a fellow director, helping introduce the five-year plan, also nursing through the new directors in the workings of a football club.

I had had three years on the board under Dan and meeting directors from other clubs so I was learning all the time.

The new board and Paul all worked closely together as one unit, it was a wonderful period.It also helps when you are winning football matches! The promotion season was fantastic and is well documented.

What a fantastic journey, the crowds, the new stands,the great buzz in the city – an amazing period which cannot be taken away no matter what happened later.

Who can forget the win at Rushden that kick-started it, the promotion at Carlisle, the title at Darlington and the celebration at the civic centre! Paul and I spent a lot of time during this period together with our families also socialising regularly. My wife Kim and Paul's wife Barbara were friends, too, and our children often played together. When Paul did his food critiquing we often joined him. We also played cricket for the TAC cricket team, a social club where the players were all rather portly.

The success brought its own problems. After winning the title in 2002 we arranged a trip to Magaluf as a reward.

I received a call on the coach on the way to the airport from Watford asking if they could speak to Paul. I told Paul about it but we left it until we returned.

Paul was thinking seriously about taking the job, they were in a higher league, better pedigree and an attraction. Paul called me to the club for a chat and I spent three hours talking to him. I thought I had dissuaded him myself but he told me later than his wife Barbara had also said no.

She had just moved down and didn't want to move again. Whatever it was, it worked and he stayed to build the next stage.

We finished eighth in division two the next season and then were going great guns in the next year when another club came calling. It was February and we were fighting at the top of the league with QPR, Swindon and Bristol City.

Phill Gill and I were driving in London on a personal business trip when Rupert Lowe the Southampton chairman rang my mobile. I had dealt with Rupert regarding getting loan players in my time on the board so was on first name terms.

He apologised sincerely but asked to speak to Paul. We were devastated but told Paul who I suspect already knew of the interest. Paul thought long and hard but thought the chance of managing in the Premiership might never come again.

We had lost our best manager with something like 10 games to go.

It was like losing your best friend or having part of you cut off – it was a massive blow.

LUGGY

We wished Paul all the best and persuaded Kevin to take over before Bobby Williamson was appointed with three games to go. Indeed Bobby's first game was against QPR, and was a title-winning game as it turned out.

Indeed that day was one of my best memories winning the title in front of a packed house at Home Park. Although the period from when Paul had left was a really nervous time, we on the board never showed it, nor did the players. They were superb.

Bobby didn't want to take any credit for this second promotion in two years, praising Luggy, as he called Paul. We all agreed that it was down to Paul, one of the most successful if not the most successful manager Plymouth Argyle had had. It had been a wonderful journey together. Paul was in the folklore of the club for what he had achieved.

Going To
The Show

PERHAPS, the look on Gordon Strachan's face and his enigmatic answer to my question, should have warned me about working with Southampton chairman Rupert Lowe.

I asked Gordon, whom I was replacing as Southampton manager in March 2004, what Rupert was like to work under.

'I'll leave that for you to find out for yourself', said the former Scotland midfielder, who took non-committal answers to an altogether different level.

And boy, did I.

I think Rupert had this idea, as I was to discover, that he thought of me as a first-team coach and not as a manager and thought he could influence me, which he found out very early on was not going to be happening.

We had a couple of discussions about the style of play and certain aspects of the game he wanted, so I knew what I was up against.

But it was a very enjoyable experience managing at Southampton and one thing I'd like to make plain at the outset is that I wasn't sacked, but found that it was impossible to prove myself and manage the club in my way under the regime at St Mary's.

So I walked away having had 13 games in charge of Saints, winning five, losing six and drawing two.

I had won two promotions with Plymouth and been named Division Three manager of the year in 2001/02 with Argyle and again Division Three manager of the year for 2003/04, so I knew I had the ability to coach and manage.

Added to which my success in turning around St Johnstone's fortunes and the experience of working under the great Jim McLean at Dundee United was a testament to my abilities.

I had also been approached by both Watford and Preston North End, while at Plymouth, before Southampton showed interest and then intent. I was offered the manager's position at Watford after an interview, with the Argyle board's permission, naturally, but wanted to finish off the job at Home Park.

I let Preston know through my agent that, thanks, but I'm not interested, but didn't have an interview.

It was a real wrench to leave Argyle after four fantastic years and with the club in the ascendancy and on the threshold of promotion for the second time in two seasons.

But, Southampton were in the Premier League and holding steady in mid-table and I realised this was the big break I was looking for.

It's what the sports fans in the United States call 'Going To The Show' – i.e. I was heading for the big time. Not only that but I figured I could improve Southampton's fortunes yet further given the time and chance to manage under my own terms.

I got neither even though I got off to a brilliant start with my first match in charge ending in a 2-0 victory over mighty Liverpool.

That was on Sunday March 14 2004 and second-half strikes from James Beattie and Kevin Phillips in front of 32,000 fans sealed the win over Stevie Gerrard's Liverpool. I could not have been happier standing on the touchline at the final whistle with the Saints supporters cheering MY team to the rafters.

But, it wasn't to last as sniping behind my back and what can only be described as the eccentric thoughts and actions of the chairman fuelled my exasperation and frustration to boiling point with me saying I couldn't go on any longer to my agent.

My agent tried to talk me out of it but I was too savvy by this stage of my career to be dissuaded.

Anyway, after the Liverpool game, Southampton went up against local rivals Portsmouth next and unfortunately we lost that match narrowly, 1-0, at Fratton Park.

I'd already experienced the animosity between Portsmouth and Southampton supporters earlier that month watching Pompey play Arsenal in the FA Cup.

Although it was a Saturday the kick-off was 6pm and as I made my way to the front doors the Portsmouth supporters spotted me as the new Southampton manager and were actually spitting on me and giving me verbal abuse as well. It was not a great moment in my life, but it gave me a timely reminder of the bad feeling between the two south coast sides. Funnily enough, it was Arsene Wenger who came to my aid and he was very upset at the treatment meted out to me and he told the stewards they should be more vigilant.

Mr Wenger said it was disgraceful that in this day and age people should be subjected to such things.

Anyway, I ended up spending around half-an-hour or so with the Arsenal manager before the game and he gave me a couple of nice tips about the league I was now in and it was an excellent conversation and very enjoyable, in marked contrast to what had gone before.

Arsenal went on to win the quarter-final tie 5-1 that night with two goals each from Thierry Henry and Freddie Ljungberg and a single goal from Kolo Toure.

It was an awesome display by Mr Wenger's team and a glimpse of the class in the Premier League and the challenge that was ahead.

After losing to Pompey, Southampton bounced back to win two in a row, Tottenham at home 1-0 and 4-1 away to Wolves, before a second loss under my management at Middlesbrough, 3-1.

The remainder of the 2003/04 Premier League season went to a similar pattern of us holding our own with a 3-1 victory at Manchester City and defeats to Bolton 2-1 and a 4-0 loss away to Chelsea.

There then followed back-to-back home draws – 1-1 with Aston Villa and 3-3 against Newcastle before rounding off that campaign with a 2-1 defeat at Charlton.

I was in charge for two matches in the 2004/05 campaign and enjoyed a 50/50 split with an opening defeat at Aston Villa and then a 3-2 win over Blackburn.

Anyway, I brought in forwards coach Kevin Summerfield who had been with me at Plymouth, but was not allowed to bring in defensive specialist John Blackley to help me on the coaching team.

I tried to force the issue of Sloop being on the coaching staff with Rupert but he was adamant and refused.

What I believe Rupert wanted was people at the club who would oversee what I was trying to achieve and in effect reporting to the chairman behind my back.

The coaches I'd inherited believed in the Southampton of the past, in a Southampton way of play which had kept them in good stead so far as staying in the Premier League was concerned.

My belief was that Southampton had to kick on and, obviously, had to adapt, to try and go forward, instead of just middling on.

I wanted to add to Southampton and the players I had in mind to recruit would move up to the next level in the manner Stoke City has done.

But I was never given the chance, as Rupert decided that there would be a committee of recruitment, with one scout looking at players in England while Terry Cooper was the club's European scout and myself and Rupert.

I became quite friendly with Terry as he was on the same wavelength as myself but when it came to meetings, it was Rupert who would try and manipulate just who he would bring to the club. That was in spite of mine and Terry's observations and ideas born out of years in the game.

I'll give you an example, we were looking for a left-back and at Rupert's insistence we went out to France to look at this certain player.

After 10 minutes I had to break the news to Rupert that the target was really a centre-half, who could play left-back as well.

But he was really ordinary as a left-back, despite the player's agent insisting to Rupert that he would be a great signing, which in my view, he wouldn't.

Terry had identified a Belgium international left-back, Jelle Van Damme, who had played for Ajax, as someone who could fill the full-back berth, while Rupert was still wanting to sign this French defender.

Another example of where Rupert's naivety caused me to miss out on a good signing was when I flew over to America to watch a target in action.

The player was only young but I fancied him and with his agent I said I wanted to sign him.

Anyway, I got a phone call during discussions with the agent from Rupert saying don't sign him, I've heard from a couple of agents that he's not good enough.

I said no, he's up to standard, having watched him from afar and in the flesh, and he's OK.

Then I said to Rupert, have you ever stopped to think why these other agents don't think this player is good enough?

Rupert said I don't know what you mean, Paul.

Well, I'll tell you why, it's because they want you to sign one of their players and not miss out on a big, fat agency fee.

But at the end of the day, you're my boss and if that's what you're wanting me to do, then fine.

That I think is when I made up my mind that Rupert and me could never work together. I just wondered why he wanted my expertise in finding him good players if he was never going to act on that advice. We came from different worlds and, really, that showed again in a pre-season training camp in Scandinavia.

We were in this magnificent hotel and facility and going through a training session when Rupert came bounding over and said he had some ideas and that if there was anything he could do, then he'd be willing to help.

I kind of fobbed him off and was supported by some of the first teamers who like me don't want someone who isn't a professional, however well meaning, trying to tell them their job.

Anyway, I said look, I really need to work on the strikers and if you want to help you can field the balls behind the net.

While he was going behind the goal I told the players, look you have my permission to miss the target as often as you want.

They smashed the balls all over the place and had the chairman racing about acting as a ball boy: it was one of several surreal moments during my spell at Southampton.

On the same trip we went for a meal to a Chinese restaurant in the square of the nearby town and the next season's fixtures had just come out and of course, all the coaching staff including Rupert were studying Southampton's forthcoming matches. Rupert, after a careful examination of the fixtures, exclaimed without so far as I could tell a smidgeon of irony: 'Well I can't see us losing a game before Christmas.'

With that, Kevin Summerfield, who had just taken a big gulp of beer, sprayed it all over the table with the comments he had just heard from the chairman. I couldn't stop myself and said to Rupert and those present, 'Forgive me for asking but are Chelsea, Liverpool, Manchester United and Arsenal no longer in this league?'

But you could never argue against Rupert or question his confidence, and he responded: 'Trust me Paul, I was a hockey player and hockey is very much like football.'

My retort was: 'Mr Chairman, no it's not, as football isn't played with a stick.'

I don't suppose that satisfied Rupert, but so far as I was concerned the debate was over.

Another of Rupert's brainwaves or ideas, if you like, was that he'd read somewhere that under-pressure players will react to different colours.

He explained that a horrible brown colour would get players down and to that effect he had the away dressing room painted totally in brown.

That way, he reasoned, the opposition players would be in a depressed frame of mind at the start of each half.

Another one of Rupert's ideas was to bring in the England rugby coach, Clive Woodward, who I think he'd known for a long time, and have him assist the players with their kicking technique.

What had happened was that sometime before I joined them, Southampton had gone out of the League Cup to Bolton on penalties, and that had annoyed Rupert so much that he wanted to do something to improve the team's kicking in dead-ball situations, like penalty shoot-outs.

There is a kind of logic as a lot of money is to be made in the latter stages of cup competitions.

I wasn't there but all the other coaches from different age groups at Southampton watched Woodward's England kicking coach try to tutor the players how to kick the ball and successfully convert a penalty.

Someone made the obvious comment after the demonstration, well that's fine, but how about trying it out when there's 20,000 staring the penalty-taker down, along with the keeper, who is also doing his best to put you off, as you prepare to take the penalty kick?

The pressure on players as they step up, even if they have the necessary technique, is immense and I don't think that had been appreciated, even though Rupert's intention had been to help.

That gives you an idea of the kind of bizarre rationale I was dealing with.

I know Summers (Kevin Summerfield) had similar experiences as me and was just as frustrated at times by what was happening.

It's no secret that many of the coaching squad were scathing of me and also Summers claiming we were trying to make changes that would threaten Southampton's success.

They were right in part as yes, we were intent on making changes but only to improve Southampton and not to the side's detriment.

Neither Summers nor myself would be manipulated which is what I believed Rupert really wanted.

At the end of the day, whatever we tried to put into practice went back to the chairman which caused ill feeling and put a strain on the whole scenario.

He'd say 'why are you doing such and such' or 'what are you reasons for making the players try these tactics in training?'

So it was pretty obvious that it was not a united front in the coaching squad.

But don't get me wrong, I was really delighted and thankful to be given the opportunity to manage at an established Premier League club. Our salaries would not be on a par with our counterparts in the Premier League, but I would have taken half my deal just to manage in the top flight.

I further alienated myself from the board when one of the directors queried my dress sense and tried to get me to 'smarten up' which I felt was a damn cheek.

I can't remember whether I actually told him to basically fuck off but he got short shrift from me and never broached the subject again.

Not that he would have much time to comment on my sartorial elegance as I was rapidly coming around to the thinking, albeit reluctantly, 'this isn't for me'.

So, with all but two matches of the 2005/06 Premier League campaign yet to be played, I let it be known I'd had enough of banging my head against a wall.

However, I let Rupert, who didn't try to stop me leaving, break the news to the media, staff and fans any way he wanted.

When I left Southampton were 10th in the league, albeit having only having played two matches, and to be fair, quite a few of the first-team squad let it be known that they were disappointed I was no longer their manager and felt I hadn't been given long enough.

So that was some comfort, but not much as both me and Summers wanted to be a success in the Premier League.

I believe that one or two of the senior players at Southampton had the ear of the chairman, and didn't like change and were staid in their ways, and didn't fancy a change of philosophy.

It seemed to me they didn't want to take a chance, were fearful of losing rather than concentrating on winning. Given time I think I could have turned Southampton into a winning team, capable of finishing in mid-table, similar to what West Ham, West Bromwich and Stoke have achieved.

Instead of which after my departure, Southampton nose-dived and were relegated at the end of the 2005/06 season.

On a personal note, the timing wasn't brilliant, either as my family had moved up on the Sunday, only for me to pack it in the following day – August 23.

The removals company were just as stunned as the football world at my decision and the guy in charge whose firm had only just brought up all our furniture from Plymouth, said he'd never known such a quick turnaround, as he prepared to shift our belongings all the way back again.

The dream for me was over and as I pondered my future with a mixture of regret and relief, the enigmatic reply of my predecessor at Southampton on the subject of working with Mr Rupert Lowe stuck in my mind. The look on Gordon Strachan's face was worth a thousand words.

I really believe that Rupert had Southampton's best interests at heart and wanted to improve their position. After all they had an excellent ground with superb training facilities and lots of good players coming through.

But it had to be done on his own terms.

At the end of the day, the experience and having to make my decision sickened me. I'd had a wee taste of life in the top flight, but felt I was happier being a Football League man and better suited to acting as a fire-fighter and reviving the fortunes of clubs, as I did next at Sheffield Wednesday.

* * * * *

Defender GRAHAM COUGHLAN, who would later team up with Sturrock, Summerfield and Blackley at Hillsborough, remembers his manager's opening match at St Mary's:

It did knock us for six, individually and collectively – we had won promotions and titles and were on the verge of going to the Championship.

Anyway, we wished him well and were glued to the TV for his first match in charge of Southampton against Liverpool.

Previously, Paul was not one to celebrate on the touchline if his team scored, he was always looking ahead to the next thing, the next play and so on.

All of us at Argyle were keen to see how he was getting on at Southampton and we were amazed to see him jumping and celebrating on the touchline at St Mary's, as his team beat Liverpool 2-0 in his first game in charge.

Paul was jumping up and down, hugging Kevin Summerfield and if he could he would have turned cartwheels – he'd won promotion and a championship title and taken Plymouth from their lowest ebb, to a division below the Premier League.

So, I phoned Paul and said what's going on here – what's with all the demonstrative celebrating?

And, he says: 'Aah, I'm in the big time now, and that's what the big-time footballers and coaches do!' He knew where I was coming from and had an answer for anything. Paul cherished his time and the opportunity to manage Southampton, it's a pity he wasn't given a longer period at the Saints.

* * * * *

KEVIN SUMMERFIELD said:

The timing of Paul's departure from Plymouth to Southampton was not ideal, but both he and I felt the team I'd inherited as caretaker-manager was solid and confident enough to withstand his departure.

I had known that Paul was very keen on moving to the Premier League and he wanted me and Sloop to join him at St Mary's at the earliest opportunity.

Sloop, for whatever reason, wasn't taken on by Southampton and stayed at Home Park, but I'd made it clear I wasn't interested in being interviewed for the manager's job at Argyle and was just happy to oversee the transition from Paul Sturrock to Bobby Williamson and, of course, promotion to the Championship.

We'll never know what might have happened if I'd said 'I'll stay at Argyle' as the opportunity to replace

Paul as manager was pretty much assured and there for me.

But you cannot turn down the opportunity to work in the Premier League, even though it never worked out for us at Southampton at the end of the day.

Sheffield Wednesday

I WAS very pleased to be appointed as manager of Sheffield Wednesday, who are with all due respect to my other teams and fans, the biggest club I have managed, certainly in terms of fan-base.

I had been out of work for around a month after severing my links with Southampton in August 2004 and was appointed Hillsborough boss in September that same year and season.

Wednesday had just been relegated into League One from the Championship and were in 17th place when I took over and definitely nobody's favourite to make an immediate return to English football's second tier.

Naturally, I was aware of Wednesday's history and importance in the league structure, after all they had reached both the FA Cup and League Cup Final in the same season, just a decade before when they were in the Premiership.

But nothing prepared me for the level of support that the club generated and the expectation and loyalty of the fans – it was awesome.

I had played and managed Dundee United, been in two World Cups with Scotland and in England recently experienced the support at both Southampton and before that Plymouth.

I knew from personal experience the Green Army at Home Park and, in particular, in away matches turned out in large numbers and, like Dundee United's Arabs, were noisily supportive, but Wednesday's fans, as I was to find out, were something else again – they were unbelievable.

After a frustrating and disappointing six-month term in charge of Southampton which ended two games into the 2004/05 Premier League season, reviving a slumbering giant like Wednesday was just the challenge I needed.

At my interview I was told that I had been given the job after a 3-1 win at Hillsborough when I was with Argyle who had battered them and that

Dundee United team photograph with Paul Sturrock front row 1998-2000 when Luggy becomes manager at long last

St Johnstone team pic plus Division One winners' trophy season 1996/97 – Sturrock's first championship success

TO
Mr Paul Sturrock

Your reference

Your correspondence of

Our reference
LDIS/

Date
12 September 2014

Dear Mr Sturrock,

The UEFA President's office referred your complaint regarding the AS Roma v Dundee United match played on 25 April 1984 to the disciplinary services unit.

In paragraph 2 of your letter to the UEFA President, Michel Platini, you clearly state: "In 2011, Riccardo Viola, son of the former President Dino Viola [president of AS Roma in 1984] disclosed that the referee of that game, Michel Vautrot, had been bribed by the Italian club. He explained how, where and when the bribe had been paid. In particular that the equivalent of £50,000 had been paid to him on the eve of the game at a local restaurant. There has, to my knowledge, never been any suggestion that this startling revelation was anything other than true".

In my capacity as Ethics and Disciplinary Inspector, I take your letter very seriously. The fight against match-fixing and any other form of corruption in football is a high priority for UEFA, which has a policy of zero tolerance towards such conduct. However, this fight must be conducted in full accordance with the legal framework in place.

As you may be aware, both the UEFA disciplinary bodies at that time rendered decisions relating to this case, on 11 June 1986 (first instance) and 2 July 1986 (Appeals body) respectively. These authorities knew about the suspicions that you raise in your letter and took all the evidence into consideration when they rendered these decisions in 1986.

It emerges from the case file that no one involved, not even Dino Viola, could identify any wrongdoing by the referee, Michel Vautrot.

First page of reply from UEFA over Paul Sturrock's attempt to have Dundee United recognition for being 'cheated' out of a European Cup Final showdown with Liverpool

Second page and signature of UEFA response from Michel Platini's office

As your letter brings no new elements or evidence to light, there is no legal basis for reopening the case. That being said, even if you did have new evidence of the alleged offence, unfortunately it would still not be possible to reopen the case because the statute of limitations at that time was ten years. The case in question is therefore closed from a disciplinary point of view.

I hope that these explanations clarify the matter for you but would be happy to answer any further questions you have in this respect.

Yours sincerely,

Jean-Samuel Leuba

Ethics and disciplinary inspector

Pictured with Scottish band Deacon Blue personnel Ricky Ross and Lorraine McIntosh who played at Paul Sturrock's testimonial celebration in 1989

With Dan McCauley, the former Plymouth Argyle owner/ chairman who had appointed Paul Sturrock as manager of the club in 2000

Pictured with Sir Bobby Charlton and Jack Charlton who along with Sir Ian Botham (not pictured) were guests at Paul Sturrock's testimonial dinner. Dundee United had played Real Sociedad (then managed by John Toshack) in a testimonial match for Paul

Press conference at Plymouth's Home Park 2007 (Paul's re-appointment as Plymouth manager). To his left is Paul Stapleton (then chairman), and fellow board members Phill Gill and Tony Wrathall (David Rowntree)

Plymouth Argyle players celebrate confirmation of promotion to what is now League One (third tier of English Football structure) at Rochdale on March 26 2002 (David Rowntree)

Paul Sturrock receives coveted manager of the month award from then Chelsea boss Claudio Ranieri, who had won the trophy the previous month (David Rowntree)

Skipper Paul Wotton and his fellow Argyle players celebrate going up as champions from then Division Three (now League Two) with 102 points, ahead of runners-up Luton Town – assistant-manager Kevin Summerfield is far right (front) (David Rowntree)

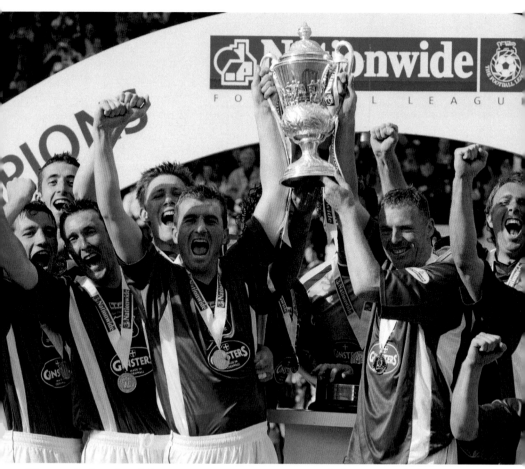

Plymouth Argyle celebrate promotion campaign and their second championship-winning title in two seasons – Paul Wotton and former Livingston centre-back Graham Coughlan holding trophy (David Rowntree)

(Left) The three amigos – Paul Sturrock flanked by his trusty lieutenants John 'Sloop' Blackley (right seated) and Kevin Summerfield (standing) in their second spell at Home Park (match versus Newcastle United). (Right) At Sheffield Wednesday, while still at Plymouth and before he was appointed Owls boss. It was this midweek match which Argyle won 3-1 that stuck in the memory of Dave Allen Sheffield Wednesday chairman to go for Sturrock when he left Southampton (David Rowntree)

With League One play-off promotion trophy in first season at Sheffield Wednesday, match played at Cardiff's Millennium Stadium (David Rowntree)

November 2007 with Plymouth Argyle chairman Paul Stapleton in Paul Sturrock's second spell as manager of the Pilgrims (David Rowntree)

With board members (left to right) Phill Gill, Paul Stapleton and Robert Dennerley (deceased) as Paul Sturrock signs contract in November 2007 confirming his second spell in charge of the Pilgrims (David Rowntree)

Paul Sturrock at full throttle as Sheffield Wednesday manager in the Owls' triumphant 4-2 play-off success over fellow promotion play-off finalists Hartlepool.

Paul Sturrock proudly displays his manager of the month award and champagne in 2002 with Plymouth Argyle (David Rowntree)

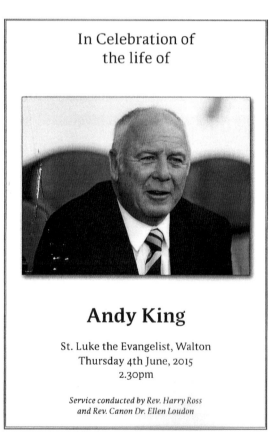

In Celebration of
the life of

Andy King

St. Luke the Evangelist, Walton
Thursday 4th June, 2015
2.30pm

*Service conducted by Rev. Harry Ross
and Rev. Canon Dr. Ellen Loudon*

Funeral of Andy King – Former Everton midfielder and Swindon Town manager, and close friend of Paul Sturrock, service held in Liverpool 2015

Unveiling of new Plymouth Argyle board (left to right) Tony Wrathall, Keith Todd, Sir Roy Gardiner (ex Manchester United chairman), Paul Stapleton, George Synan and Robert Dennerley. (David Rowntree)

At Southend United with first-team coach Graham Coughlan

Plymouth Argyle midfielder Carl Fletcher has hands on hips after Marcel Seip (on loan to Blackpool) celebrates scoring against his employers at Bloomfield Road in 2-0 victory for the Seasiders (David Rowntree)

Carl Fletcher pictured giving the Argyle board an ironic thumbs up at Home Park after scoring against Ipswich Town (David Rowntree)

An embarrassed Plymouth Argyle chairman Paul Stapleton looks on while his wife Kim and daughter Lucy celebrate son-in-law and husband, respectively, Marcel Seip's goal against his own club for Blackpool, which infuriated the Argyle players and travelling Green Army (Plymouth fans) and became known as 'Thumbsgate'. (David Rowntree)

had really impressed the Sheffield board. A lot of supporters mentioned that to me, too, when I first took over at Wednesday, just how good a performance Plymouth had put on that time.

That was key and as I said I was very pleased that people had recognised the job I had done with Plymouth and clearly were hoping that I could do the same for my new club, who had just been relegated.

I replaced former boss Chris Turner in the hot seat on September 23, and brought in my coaches Kevin Summerfield and John Blackley, both of whom I had worked with successfully before.

Before being taken on at Sheffield I had been invited by Wednesday chairman, Dave Allen, to meet up with other members of the board and watch his side, then under the temporary charge of caretaker coach and former Plymouth Argyle defender, Mark Smith, in a League Cup tie at Coventry City, which the visitors lost 1-0.

Mark Smith had played under Dave Smith at Home Park in the late eighties and was a youth coach at Wednesday and was to have just the one game in charge.

I met the chairman, Dave Allen, and director, Barry Gold, along with my agent at a hotel in the centre of Coventry and we shook hands on the deal.

My first game was away to Wrexham which we won quite convincingly 3-0 with goals from Steve MacLean, Chris Brunt and Adam Proudlock.

I had changed the system of play before and during that game at the Racecourse and my tactics worked which allowed me to judge the players I had and how they'd react.

It was a pleasing start but key to me was to improve Wednesday's home form as they were getting huge crowds but not satisfying an exasperated fan-base.

Having a fervent and expectant home crowd in large numbers is great but can be a double-edged sword, as the pressure was clearly getting to some of the players.

Wednesday had already lost a number of home fixtures that season in both the league and cup competitions, so changing that mindset from a negative to a positive was high on my agenda. Over the next few weeks, it was a curate's egg in terms of results, wins interspersed with draws and defeats, but Wednesday enjoyed a good Christmas and new year going undefeated until the middle of February when we lost 2-1 at home to Bradford City.

But, most encouragingly, that little run had seen us climb into the play-off positions where we lay in fourth position.

Our captain Lee Bullen and leading goal-scorer Steven MacLean, whom I was later to sign for Plymouth without enjoying the same level of success, were big players for Wednesday, but I needed to move players on and also freshen up the squad with loans, if necessary.

I had brought in young Irish defender Joey O'Brien on loan from Bolton and he scored on his debut, while I managed to borrow Kenwyne Jones, initially as a centre-half from Harry Redknapp, who was now managing Southampton.

I talked to Harry on the phone about Kenwyne who had been a youth player at St Mary's but wasn't convinced his future lay as a centre-back and felt as a big lad he would be a bigger threat as a striker. I didn't feel Kenwyne sensed danger as a defender but I needed a big target man and asked Harry if he would mind if I tried him out as a striker.

Harry, bless him, said no problem, go for it and I then had to convince Kenwyne that I felt his future was as a striker not a defender.

In all, Kenwyne played seven games for us and scored seven goals but his successful transformation from defence to attack had not gone unnoticed and Harry brought him back to Southampton in the January, where he started to get involved there, too.

A Trinidad and Tobago boy, Kenwyne was quick over 10 yards and could jump the highest of any player on the books and had all the attributes to be a massive player for us.

However, in his first game for us he didn't look the part of a big target man with height and pace, and he was clearly lacking in confidence.

But once he'd scored, and that was a bit of a fluke after the Doncaster Rovers goalkeeper had gifted him the goal, Kenwyne didn't look back.

O'Brien also had to go back to Bolton as he had picked up an injury so I brought in a lad called Craig Rocastle, whose uncle, David, had played for Arsenal.

Craig was on Chelsea's books and definitely had attributes and promise and had his best game for us in the play-off final at the Millennium Stadium.

I also brought in another young prospect and son of a famous footballer, Alex Bruce, whose dad, Steve, had a phenomenal career with Manchester United.

Alex came as a utility player from Birmingham on loan, essentially as a centre-back, but I played him at full-back, and he helped us put together a solid defence with a settled line-up of Lee Bullen, Paul Heckingbottom, Richard Wood and Patrick Collins.

Bruce, though, was sent off on his debut against Hudderfield which had we won instead of losing 1-0, would have taken us up into third position in the league.

So, that didn't augur well, but thereafter Alex was an important figure for us.

Lee's contribution both as a player, in a position of centre-half where due to injury I had converted him, and also as an inspirational captain was fantastic.

Goalkeeper David Lucas was also an important player for me during that time, while a young lad called Jon-Paul McGovern, who had been at Celtic, made the most of his opportunity playing wide right.

Rocastle was on the other flank, with Whelan and Brunt in the centre of midfield, with Steve MacLean, Lee Peacock, Drew Talbot and James Quinn up front.

Essentially, though, we had a young and perhaps naive squad of players, who nonetheless were adaptable, receptive and hungry for success, despite the necessary mix-and-match approach at times.

Well, anyway, we came to the penultimate game of the regular season and needed to win away at Hull City in order to guarantee our play-off place.

Hull were already promoted in the automatic positions, and we had been leading 1-0 through Talbot but let in City who had equalised and were battering us as the match entered its final few minutes.

I've always had a superstition about not being pitchside in injury time, so I made my way to the dressing room preparing the rant I was about to unleash on the players.

When they trooped in looking suitably hot and exhausted, it was the end of April after all, I let rip saying how can you think of promotion when you've let a lead slip away in that fashion, when you know a draw is not really going to be enough?

Hull are already in the Championship and we're very, very close: it was that kind of thing, blah, blah, blah and all the while Stevie Adams, who had been with me at Argyle, was trying to catch my attention.

I ignored Stevie at first and finished off cursing the players, until he whispered in my ear, 'Gaffer, we scored a winner in the last minute.'

To say that I felt stupid is a massive understatement – I should have been congratulating the lads for a 2-1 win and not berating them. Quinn scored the winner, by the way.

We lost our final game of the regular season 3-2 at home to Bristol City but really all the players were looking toward the Brentford game in west London as were the nearly 30,000 fans who were at Hillsborough.

Our opponents in the promotion play-offs finished up in fourth place, one position higher than ourselves and we knew that we would have to be solid and focused against a good Brentford side.

We finished up winning the first leg at Hillsborough 1-0 through a McGovern goal, but Brentford were perhaps unlucky not to have scored themselves and went into the second leg confident of turning us over.

The players were edgy going into the second semi-final as were the fans but I just tried to settle them down by saying I'd give anything to be in their place, rather than watching from the dug-out.

It was far from a Churchillian call to arms, in fact, my pre-match rhetoric consisted largely of me poking fun at myself, but I think it eased the tension.

The lads won the tie 2-1 and 3-1 on aggregate, goals from Peacock and Brunt sending Wednesday into a play-off final against Hartlepool in Cardiff.

So against all the odds and early-season predictions, Sheffield Wednesday were one result away from an instant return to the Championship.

And if there was any doubt over the passion and level of belief among the Wednesday fans, then our magnificent turn-out in a near-60,000 attendance ended all sensible debate.

There were 41,000 Sheffield Wednesday supporters in the final attendance figure of 59,808 souls, which still makes my head spin just to think of it.

Hartlepool came to the party with a caretaker manager, Martin Scott, in charge and having played well all season, finishing one point behind our 72-point total and having won two more games than we had.

Anyway in the lead-up to the final, we had two weeks basically from the win at Brentford to the Millennium in which to keep ourselves fit and occupied.

Before the Brentford game, just to break the ice and relax the players, we had taken them out on the beer where they could drink as much as they liked.

There didn't seem much point in just focusing on the job at hand and the let-your-hair-down session seemed to do the trick, as the camaraderie among the players increased as their tension eased.

So ahead of the final, we had taken the lads out canoeing on a man-made lake which they seemed to enioy and as the match approached we did nothing other than what we usually would in preparation for any upcoming match.

What I didn't want to do was to over-emphasise the importance of the game and put pressure on the players.

Hartlepool, who had beaten Tranmere Rovers on penalties in their semi-final, were in Cardiff a day ahead of us and presumably trying to do the same as us, just relax.

There would be enough pressure in the final and the match which I felt was a very good encounter between two fine sides.

We had travelled down to Cardiff the night before the final and a good many Wednesday supporters had already made their way there and the noise was unbelievable.

On the day of the match we went as a group for a wee walk around, a light training session and off we went for the game.

In the first half we were dominant and took the lead right on half-time through McGovern.

I should also mention it was the warmest day I've ever spent at a football match, at pitchside it was absolutely roasting and most of the action in the second half was at our end of the pitch.

Both sets of players were absolutely drenched in sweat and I had gone through five bottles of water alone in the first half.

At the break, I told the players however tired you're feeling they are 1-0 down and so will be doubly-knackered.

Thinking I'd done a good job at rallying the troops, that positivity swiftly vanished as Hartlepool scored twice after the break and were the more confident side in the second period and leading 2-1 going into the closing stages.

But that's football for you, just when you think everything's going to plan, fate comes back to bite you big time.

Anyway, we were 2-1 down and making no inroads into changing that scoreline so I decided to make a triple substitution.

I brought on Steve MacLean, who had been sidelined with a broken toe for quite a few weeks, and had been sitting on the subs' bench.

Steve had been a catalyst for Sheffield Wednesday before his injury and hadn't really trained for several weeks, so it was a bit of a shot in the dark.

But I'd decided I'd had enough of this, we were trailing 2-1, so on came MacLean, Talbot and Collins with about 17 minutes to go to the final whistle.

The re-jig worked as Hartlepool gave away a penalty with less than 10 minutes to go and lost a player in the process as Talbot was deemed to be in a goalscoring position when he was brought down.

Then there was a debate over who would take the penalty which would take the tie into extra-time.

Well, MacLean had no doubt that it was going to be him: he was leading goalscorer and needed just one more goal to amass 20 goals for the season and also net a £20,000 bonus for reaching that tally.

So, there was no chance of anyone getting the ball off him, and he duly despatched the penalty which sent us into extra-time against a 10-man Hartlepool.

But, really, I think had they still had 11 on the pitch, the outcome wouldn't have been any different as our tails were up and we deservedly took the lead in extra-time with a great goal from Whelan.

Talbot put the result beyond doubt when he rounded the Pools keeper in the last minute of extra-time for a 4-2 victory.

Wednesday had gone back up in double-quick time and in 2005/06 they would be playing in the Championship where we would meet up with Mr Lowe's Southampton, who had been relegated from the Premier League.

Job done as far as I was concerned.

The celebration scene was incredible with the noise from the Wednesday fans absolutely deafening and the players' families all there trying to take it all in.

The coach journey back from Cardiff to Sheffield was also unbelievable and the celebrations continued despite our progress being impeded by roadworks and the resultant traffic jam.

A lot of the boys had been sinking beer like there's no tomorrow and inevitably needed the toilet and wanted to get out at the next service station.

But for me, I was looking ahead to the next year when my job would be to keep the club up while everybody else was dancing up and down around the bus. I was in a world of my own.

Meanwhile, the lads were doing the can-can, dancing between the cars and being joined by the supporters and on a real high. We managed to get all the players back on the coach and the driver concluded that the quickest way of reaching the next service station would be to drive on the hard shoulder.

So, he drove, illegally, down the hard shoulder for six or seven miles, but reached the services without further incident.

That is until at least four or five thousand Wednesday fans – I kid you not – spotted the players and were all dancing the can-can up the escalators to the toilets which were on the upper level.

It was a really great moment when players and fans were as one in support of their team. It is a football moment I will never forget.

After the proverbial Lord Mayor's show, I had to come back down to earth and make decisions on some of the boys' futures. It's heartbreaking when you see lads who had been celebrating just a couple of days' earlier, fighting back the tears, after being released.

But that's all part of management and I had to make those kind of decisions on the basis of which players would be best suited to keeping us in the Championship, for although we had won promotion and had a fabulous fan-base, money was still tight.

Getting promoted was the icing on the cake, I'll never lose sight of that achievement.

And the following year I do believe I did a good job, too, in keeping Sheffield Wednesday in the Championship, which as I've always emphasised is probably harder to achieve than winning promotion in the first place.

Wednesday were 10 points clear of the third and final relegation place at the end of the campaign, but our safety wasn't assured until the last few matches when we lost just once in nine games.

One of the most memorable matches came in the league clash with Millwall in mid-February where we lost our goalkeeper through injury early on. I've a well-known reputation for not having a keeper among the substitutes, so I had to put Lee Bullen, our skipper, in goal.

At half-time, all the players were concerned with how we would survive the next 45 minutes without a recognised goalkeeper. Millwall, as anyone will tell you, is not an easy place to play at with a full squad and at the best of times.

So, I said to them, look, if you win this match you'll be heroes and if you lose then it's my fault for not having a goalkeeper on the bench, so at the end of the day you've got nothing to worry about.

We went ahead in the first 10 minutes of the second half with a goal from Frank Simek which angered both Millwall's players and their fans, because the home team felt they should have been given a free kick earlier.

The banter had been good-natured up until that point, but after that it was mayhem. We won the game 1-0, but after the match the home fans beat up one of our directors and also damaged the coach.

It was a scary time and just shows what you have to go through sometimes to get a result.

Anyway, ahead of the 2006/07 Championship season, I was told by the chairman that the budget was going to be cut and that he wanted me to have the side play a more open style of football.

He'd rather lose 3-2 and than draw 0-0, he said, whereas I countered saying that we didn't have the money to bring that kind of player to the club.

This led to a debate between the chairman and myself about which players he wanted to be released which led to a vote on the board and a furious row ending in me swearing a good deal as I left them in no doubt over my opposition to their plan and interference.

Anyway, the strangest thing happened – I was offered an extension to my contract just a week before I was sacked. That was in October 2006 and I still can't see for the life of me just how that made any sense, business or otherwise.

When it was known I'd been axed around 3,000 Wednesday fans gathered at the club to show their appreciation of me.

My last match in charge was in the 4-0 defeat at Colchester on October 18.

That was another fantastic moment at a great football club and like I said earlier, the biggest I've been involved at and proud to have managed.

* * * * *

KEVIN SUMMERFIELD believes working at Sheffield Wednesday provided the perfect antidote to the disappointment he and Sturrock both felt after their experience at Southampton.

Taking over at Sheffield Wednesday was the perfect fit for us and reminded me of the times at Plymouth. The club was different and the people were different and we were confident we could do a good job there.

It would have been great to have stayed at Wednesday for a longer period, but such is the way with the modern-

day game that if the results don't go in your favour then you're out on your ear.

But we were not out of work for, just as we went to Wednesday very quickly after leaving Southampton, so Swindon came knocking.

That, of course, was down to Paul's reputation, he was definitely a wanted man and he wanted the people around him he could trust.

In terms of what we achieved at Sheffield Wednesday in gaining promotion from League One and consolidating their position in the Championship, I don't think the club has done any better since then, have they?

I know Paul still thinks that was one of his better jobs and that play-off final for drama and euphoria will stay long in all our memories. It was a fantastic experience.

* * * * *

JOHN 'SLOOP' BLACKLEY echoes his fellow Scot's affirmation of the immense support Wednesday's play-off final generated and his pride at helping the Owls achieve it.

It was the greatest day of my life when we went to Cardiff for the play-off final against Hartlepool.

The fans were fantastic and really got behind us on the run-in to the play-offs and at the final were just incredible. We were really what I would term, a working, league side and had come up on the rails to reach the final, but the supporters were appreciative of the hard work that had taken us into the top five, just one season after being relegated.

We had beaten Brentford over two legs which was a remarkable achievement and for the play-off final the support was tremendous and if we ever needed reminding of just how big Sheffield Wednesday Football Club is, that day at the Millennium Stadium removed all doubt. So as far as I'm concerned, it was the best day – ever.

The key again was Paul's meticulous preparations and insistence on training and fitness and the players responded by doing everything that was asked of them. And that was to go out and win football matches.

* * * * *

BLACKLEY also recounts how his switch from Plymouth to Sheffield left him with a guilty conscience, as the defensive coach explains:

I wasn't surprised that Paul went to Southampton when the opportunity arose as he had built up a terrific reputation as a coach and manager at Argyle, and clearly deserved a shot at the top flight in English football.

And it was only right that Kevin Summerfield went with him to Southampton, as they had led Argyle to the brink of a second, successive promotion in two years.

I stayed on at Plymouth to work alongside the new Argyle manager, Bobby Williamson, who oversaw Argyle's promotion as title winners into what is now the Championship.

Bobby had asked me to stay on at Plymouth and I agreed, but after Paul left Southampton and was appointed manager of Sheffield Wednesday, he asked me to join him at Hillsborough.

I felt really awkward because I'd told Bobby I'd stay and help him at Plymouth but Paul wanted me, too, at Sheffield. And in my heart of hearts I knew where I wanted to be.

And so I went to Sheffield to be with Paul and Kevin, but letting Bobby down has always played on my conscience, as I left Argyle under something of a cloud I suppose, from my own point of view.

There is no doubt in my mind and with all due respect to Southampton who were and still are a top-flight club, Sheffield Wednesday is the biggest club I've ever been at and the supporters are different class.

* * * * *

GRAHAM COUGHLAN who was to rejoin Sturrock at Wednesday in July 2005 from Plymouth Argyle recalls making the trip across the Severn Bridge to Cardiff for the final. He said:

Paul did an unbelievable job up here at Sheffield Wednesday, who were in the doldrums and dropped into League One, and were long odds to get back up into the first tier of the Football League when Paul was appointed.

So, to get a club promoted that year via the play-offs was fantastic and proved once again that Paul Sturrock is a genius when it comes to strategy and planning a campaign.

At the end of the campaign, Wednesday had finished fifth with 72 points, but brilliantly had extended their season and given their massive and devoted fan-base the chance of returning back to the Championship.

I went up to watch Wednesday in the second play-off semi-final against Brentford at Griffin Park, with another pal of Paul's from Plymouth and former player, Alan Rogers.

Wednesday had won the first leg 1-0 and then did the double over Brentford with a 2-1 victory, which put them into the play-off final against Hartlepool, who'd beaten Tranmere on penalties.

The atmosphere in Sheffield was incredible and at the Millennium Stadium on May 29, 2005, in front of nigh-on 60,000 fans against Hartlepool, Paul delivered up the win for the Wednesday fans.

A group of us from Plymouth had travelled via minibus to Cardiff and watched Wednesday win a nail-biting final 4-2 after extra time.

If ever anyone had reservations about Paul Sturrock's abilities as a coach and manager before that remarkable day in May, he'd removed them big time.

Yes, he'd managed in the Premier League with Southampton, but with all due respect, Wednesday are a huge club, both in expectation and tradition and Paul had weaved his magic.

So to manage, back-to-back Southampton in the Premier League and then Sheffield Wednesday and restore their fortunes, is remarkable, and shows he's more than capable of managing at that level.

Some people might debate Paul's ability, but I'd debate with them every day of the week, because I know from first-hand experience, that he has left clubs in a far better position than when he joined them.

That is a credo he has always preached to me: 'Make sure you leave a football club in a better position than when you signed – then you know you've done your job properly.'

That's something I've taken on board, whether it's improving results and the infrastructure, make certain you can leave with your head held high.Needless, to say, Paul remains a very, very popular man in Sheffield among Wednesday fans.

I still live up here in Sheffield and can vouch that Paul is idolised by the Wednesday supporters to this day.

* * * * *

GUY BRANSTON, experienced defender and now chief scout at Notts County recalls his time with Sturrock at Hillsborough:

The first thing you've got to recognise is that Paul Sturrock is an excellent coach and manager, his record of success at football clubs proves that.

Unfortunately, I did not get a chance to spend long with him at Sheffield Wednesday, but the way he got them promoted via the play-offs was outstanding.

I believe my time at Sheffield Wednesday, brief though it was, was the best of my footballing life.

Wednesday are a massive club and their supporters are fantastic.

I've always tried to be me and not what others think I should be and plain speaking, which is probably why I've had a few run-ins at various clubs. I came to Wednesday after being signed by our then manager, Chris Turner, in 2004 and felt I was in good form for the Owls, then in League One after our relegation from the Championship.

My big regret is not being able to prove myself to Paul, who replaced Chris Turner, although I felt our sound defence had laid the platform for what turned out to be a promotion-winning campaign.

Soaring With Swindon

WELL, I wasn't unemployed for very long, I think around 10 days or so, before I accepted an approach to join Swindon Town.

That would have been around the early part of November, Swindon having allowed Dennis Wise and his deputy, Gus Poyet, to join Leeds United.

As I remember Swindon were around third or fourth in League Two and the move was so quick that I didn't have time to see them play or run the rule over the squad I was to inherit.

Summers and Sloop came with me, so it was an almost seamless transition from Sheffield to

Swindon, which again kept the continuity of my coaching team intact.

I met the owner, Mr Seton Wills, who was part of the tobacco company, but the guy who was running the club was a Mr Mike Diamandis, who was the general manager at Swindon, with Martyn Starnes as the chief executive.

Martyn would later assume the same role at Plymouth Argyle.

When I got to Swindon, they were in a healthy position and the management team of Dennis Wise and Gus Poyet had done very well.

I also had some good players on the playing staff, and so I had a reasonable squad to work with.

Christian Roberts, who could play on the wing and also as a striker, was already there and I strengthened the Swindon squad by bringing in Lee Peacock from Sheffield Wednesday and also Barry Corr, who had also been with me at Hillsborough.

As I've said Swindon were a nice, well-managed, friendly club, who were clearly ambitious and keen to gain promotion and because of my successful track record in that department, welcomed me on board.

One of the first things that struck me, though, was the antipathy between the Swindon fans and

Diamandis, who was a hate figure for the supporters. I had a few meals with him and on the social side he seemed to be a nice enough man but the fans did not like Diamandis one little bit.

But, I was able to bring in a few more players who I believed would help with the transition and enable Swindon to achieve their ambition of gaining promotion to League One.

I was only at Swindon for just over a year, but quite a lot happened during that short period – we gained promotion and all the while there were rumblings and rumours about a consortium takeover.

Sir Seton Wills had ploughed millions into the club, decided he'd had enough and would be selling up. But I just kept my head down and only got involved with potential suitors when they came my way.

My brief, so far as I was concerned, was to have the final word on anything to do with players who would be coming in. That was to be my sole concern.

Anyway, a bit later on when the club had been taken over by a consortium, that was to be tested in what I can only describe as farcical circumstances.

What happened was there was a proposed takeover by a Portuguese consortium and they made a good offer to the Wills family, who were starting to feel the pinch.

As I remember it now the offer was made through a Portuguese agent, Jose Veiga, with a guy called Jorge Rubinstein, who was his British-based advisor.

On paper, it was a great offer and the Wills family would have got a high percentage of their investment in Swindon back.

However, there was a catch. The Portuguese wanted to take over the day-to-day running of the football club, and basically bring in a lot of young, Portuguese footballers, who had played for Sporting Lisbon under-19s.

It was all kind of vague, so far as I was concerned, but I think the plan was to bring these young players in and improve them and acquaint them with League Two and League One football.

But they would have to meet certain criteria before finalising the deal and taking over the football club.

I must add that they didn't put one penny into Swindon while all this was going on.

The potential buyers wanted to bring in three Portuguese players, one of whom had played in the Spanish first division.

I wasn't at all happy with this scenario but I didn't want to do anything which would have posed a threat to Mr Wills getting a lot of his money back.

The deal hinged on these players being allowed to sign for Swindon Town.

So, I was between a rock and a hard place so far as that was concerned and I agreed even though I was contracted to have sole discretion on player recruitment.

My other concern was the wage structure at Swindon and I didn't want the recruitment of the new influx of these players to threaten that arrangement.

One of the trio, a defender, had actually played in this country for Accrington Stanley and I found out that he had been on £500 a week, while his new salary would be £2,500 a week.

So, that was already going to be a problem, that and the fact they weren't really at the standard we were looking for.

Nevertheless, out of respect to Mr Wills, I agreed to let the Spanish striker play for us in a JPT cup tie and he scored a good goal, in a game we won comfortably. But other than that the boy didn't get involved.

The three amigos as they were tagged by the fans were Mauro Almeida, Ibon Arrieta and Franklin Anzite.

I never played the other two imports, although there were plenty more in the pipeline.

At the same time as all that was happening, on a pre-season tour to Austria, just about every day a trialist would turn up at the training ground and every one of them seemed to be about 5ft 6in, winger size, and would get walked over in the physical demands of English football.

They weren't bad players and had a modicum of ability, it's just they would have got trampled on and so I refused to take them on, much to the disgust of the so-called new owners, who thought these trialists would all become stars. And all this as I was attempting to recruit for the 2007/08 season in League One. It's one thing gaining promotion, it's an even bigger job keeping your side up.

Jorge's next trick was to bring in Rufus Brevett as technical director, whose job was to find players and bring them to me. But so far as I was concerned he was the middle man between me and the board and that was it, which he reported back to his employers.

So far as I could tell, Rufus, who had played for Queens Park Rangers and Fulham as a full-back, was given the post when Jorge had found out he had been a footballer from chatting while they picked up their children, who went to the same school.

Anyway, one day Jorge dragged me into his office where members of the board were present to tell me of a brilliant target he had uncovered and wanted us to sign.

I was told the target had been a top player for Ajax and played several times for them.

The player himself had incurred a bad knee injury and was released by Ajax after playing second division football in the Netherlands.He had a pedigree of sorts but hadn't played to a high standard for two or three years, but that didn't stop them raving about him and how we couldn't miss out on signing him, as he's just the kind of player we want.

I looked around the room and said well, I've got just the sort of player we want in my office right now, and they all looked very interested.

I continued, he's played 550 games, played in two World Cups and scored 150 goals, and they said yes that's the type of player we need, who is it? And I said, it's me. Once things had calmed down I said look, it means absolutely nothing having a great CV and reading all about him.

Anyway, I brought the player in and he couldn't run because of the cruciate knee injury and wouldn't have passed a medical, let alone a ball. So, that didn't go down very well and me telling Rufus what his job was going to be.

I was starting to become very disenchanted by the state of affairs and I couldn't really care less whether I stayed or not.

So on a matchday, the proposed new chairman comes in and is giving me the big one about what he's going to do at Swindon and what we're going to achieve, blah, blah, blah.

Apparently, he couldn't speak or understand English and all this was being interpreted by a Scots girl, who happened to be a nanny in his employ.

So, wishing I was anywhere else on the planet, once his selling pitch had finished, I said to the young lass, tell him what I'm about to tell you and nothing else, OK?

She said what is it you want me to say and I said, 'Just tell him why doesn't he fuck off!'

She did, but he understood better English than he was letting on and he smiled even before she'd finished translating.

He saw the funny side of my response but I knew my time was running short at Swindon.

So, when the offer came to return to Plymouth and manage the club I'd also had great success with, there was only ever going to be one answer.

I left the County Ground for Home Park practically a year after I took over the Swindon reins and as I always attempt to achieve, I packed my bags knowing I'd left them in a better place than when I'd found them.

I had a win ratio of 50 per cent in my tenure at Swindon and the club were in a healthy position in League One. I had always prided myself on a good win ratio, which I generally achieved – the rare exceptions being at Dundee United and in my second spell at Plymouth.

I had also left them in the capable hands of Dave 'Budgie' Byrne, who was a successful caretaker manager before Maurice Malpas was appointed manager later in the 2007/08 season.

There was also good news at Swindon in the 2007/08 League One season, with the club, in peril of falling into administration, being taken over by a consortium led by Andrew Fitton for an undisclosed fee from Sir Seton Wills, which cleared the debt and removed the transfer.

But before I sign off from my Swindon spell, I must tell you the story of one of the players, whose appetite for the game summed up the spirit at the club and was both touching and humbling.

Barry Corr had been with me at Sheffield Wednesday and one of the first players I brought to Swindon when I could. Now it was reaching the end of my first season in charge and we were on the brink of winning promotion.

Barry, as it transpired, had a stress fracture of the spine, but wanted to play on with it. He might have finished up without feeling in his leg or worse.

I said to Barry, look the doctor has refused to let you play because it is too risky and left him out of the game, the second last of the season, away to Bristol Rovers.

We'd been on a good run but we lost at Rovers, 1-0, and in the dressing room afterwards, Barry collared me and said, look gaffer, I'm desperate to play in our last match at home to Walsall.

Barry had played several weeks unknown to us with this condition and said to me: I'll sign anything to free the club from any responsibility – I just really want to play for Swindon in this match.

But the doctor was adamant and it was heartbreaking to turn him down. It brought it home to me just how important football was to people, that they would put their future wellbeing at risk.

LUGGY

KEVIN SUMMERFIELD claims gaining promotion with Swindon was a tougher task than many football fans have given the coaching team credit for. He said:

That was the hardest promotion really because Swindon had the weakest squad overall in terms of the division they were in (League Two). So to galvanise a squad of players in the six or seven months we were there, I'd say we did really well.

Also Paul is very good at dealing with situations like we had at Swindon with the potential takeover as a continuing backdrop to our league campaign and as coaches we just got on with it.

Paul was excellent at dealing with the powers that be and talking them around to his way of thinking and ultimately I think we left Swindon in a stronger position with a stronger squad than the one we inherited.

I think myself, Sloop and Paul were confident that Swindon team could have competed in the league above. So we were happy that we'd achieved that and if Plymouth hadn't come along then I doubt we'd had left them for many other jobs.

SOARING WITH SWINDON

* * * * *

MARTYN STARNES as chief executive of Swindon Town during that period, watched at first hand Sturrock's winning mentality and ability to transcend the politicking at the Wiltshire club over the course of a difficult season and secure promotion for the Robins.

After a pre-season tour of Austria where the Portuguese consortium (BEST Holdings) sent a number of trialists, they wanted three players signed by Swindon.

The trio concerned were one Portuguese called Almeida and Spaniard named Arrieta and another player called Anzite, who was from France.

The players were all paid excellent wages for the division and had 1m Euro exit clauses in their contracts which were never going to be realised. They weren't good enough for League Two let alone attract interest from other clubs that would pay any sort of fee.

The consortium bizarrely appointed an American guy called Jim Little as chairman. This was all done before the Portuguese signed any form of contract with the Wills family or introduced any funds.

Soon after his 'appointment' Jim held a meeting with Paul and myself and said to Paul: 'It's quite simple.

All you have to do is win football matches and make money.'

I thought Paul was going to explode and I tried to kick him under the table to distract his response. But he caught my eye and responded by asking Jim whether he had a magic wand up his sleeve.

He'd need it if his simple objective was certain to succeed. By this time Paul and I both knew we wouldn't be staying at Swindon under this regime and we were both looking out for other opportunities.

Paul went back to Plymouth and soon after I left to go to Yeovil. But I really enjoyed the craic and sense of community that Paul and the coaching team managed to engender in the year he was with us at Swindon.

An example of Paul's ascerbic wit, I recall, was the manager's estimation of the talents or otherwise of one of his players.

On Christian Roberts, Paul once said that the player could be Premier League but only for five minutes a game. The other 85 minutes he was only Conference.

During the time at Swindon, Paul shared a house with Kevin Summerfield, John Blackley, Dave Byrne and his son Blair Sturrock. Up to three nights a week physio Dick Mackey acted as head chef and prepared three-course meals for all of us with help from the others. They were fun evenings where we would watch football on the TV and talk about Swindon and the game generally.

Every Friday before a home game we would all go out for a meal at Fabio's in Swindon Old Town and Paul became quite well known to the staff there.

As ever, Paul stamped his personality on the club, taking an interest in everything that was going on and talking to all the staff including the guys who ran the Community operation.

He decorated his own office in all his former club colours and even refurbed the dressing room kitchen area for the bald-headed 'Curly' who made the teas on matchday for the management, players and officials as a surprise birthday present.

* * * * *

DAVID BYRNE, who remained at Swindon, despite the offer to rejoin Sturrock, Summerfield and Blackley at Home Park, enjoyed the experience. He said:

When Paul came in to Swindon he asked me to join up with Sloop and Summers on the coaching staff, which I was delighted to do.

Paul's brief to me was help bring the youth department up to speed and bring some likely youngsters through for first-team consideration.

He had a group of people around him that he knew and trusted, leaving him to get on with his job of getting Swindon promoted.

Which is exactly what he did.

Paul's success record as a manager is already well documented, but I don't think you could play down what he achieved in the face of difficult circumstances off the pitch Swindon. The proposed takeover by a Portuguese group, which Rufus Brevett was part of, was an absolute shambles and they tried to interfere or influence which players would benefit Swindon. Those of us lucky enough to know Paul, will know how far they got with that enterprise.

Fortunately, they didn't succeed and eventually Andrew Fitton and his consortium brought stability to the club, but Swindon had already won promotion under Paul.

Like Harry Redknapp and Dave Jones, Paul has proved himself as someone who can work successfully under the constraints of a small budget.

And now I'm working with Paul again, at Yeovil Town, and as with the other times we've been together, I never had a moment's hesitation in accepting his offer.

* * * * *

JOHN BLACKLEY remembers leaving south Yorkshire for Wiltshire where the coaching team of Sturrock, Summerfield and Blackley were to weave their magic again.

After the power struggle and frustration at Sheffield, Swindon was the next port of call for us and Paul was appointed manager very swiftly after leaving Hillsborough.

Again, Swindon were a nice club with very nice people running it and again we managed to win promotion to League One with Swindon and like at Sheffield Wednesday at the first time of asking.

I think Paul was appointed as manager in November and me and Kevin followed, but a few matches had been played already.

Swindon finished third at the end of the 2006/07 season, so we were in an automatic promotion position, so there was no heart-stopping moments as with Wednesday in the play-offs.

Plymouth Argyle – The Second Time Around

WHERE to start on my return to Plymouth Argyle, that doesn't further support the stock saying of 'never go back'?

And yet I did, along with Summers and Sloop, and we all thought that we were doing the right thing, after all we'd had great success and times at the club with promotions and a spirit of enterprise, so to speak which found Plymouth in the Championship.

I took over from Ian Holloway in November 2007 who had joined Leicester City, and to be fair, he'd left a good squad of players behind for his successor.

Apparently, the chairman of Swindon Town, where I was still the boss, had told Paul Stapleton that he'd been expecting a phone call from Plymouth as soon as he heard of Holloway's departure from Home Park.

However, I was contracted still at Swindon and in lieu of compensation we agreed that I would forego the wages owed to me, as part of the deal.

Swindon had a cash-flow problem and the shambles of the aborted Portuguese takeover didn't help any, but fortunately Andrew Fitton assumed control in early 2008 and matters stabilised at the Wiltshire outfit.

That was a comfort as we'd had a good year at Swindon and got them promoted which was pleasing and left the club well-placed in League One.

Perhaps, I should have given it more thought about returning to Argyle, maybe it was a case of my heart ruling my head. I don't know, it's easy to look back and be wise, isn't it?

I considered the Argyle chairman, Paul Stapleton, to be a personal friend and we had enjoyed a very good working relationship together the first time around and also kept in touch regularly when I left to join Southampton, then Sheffield Wednesday and Swindon.

The Argyle board had allowed me to recruit players I believed would move the club forward and didn't interfere. They had trust in my judgement and I had no reason to doubt that would be the case when I re-joined Plymouth in the wake of Holloway joining Leicester toward the end of November.

Myself, Sloop and Summers took over officially on November 27 and by the end of the 2007/08 season we'd achieved Plymouth's highest finish in the second tier of English football.

We finished 10th having been in the play-offs at one stage and, again at one stage, had a good squad of players, well for a while.

However, we lost leading goal-scorer Sylvan Ebanks-Blake to Wolves for £1.5million early in January 2008. He was followed by youth product Dan Gosling a week later, on January 15, to Everton for a cool £2million and David 'Chuck' Norris right at the end of the same month to Ipswich Town again for a deal amounting to £2million.

Chuck had been a fantastic servant to Argyle and the transfer allowed him to move back to an area near to where he was brought up. I cannot speak highly enough of Chuck, his ability and his loyalty over the six years or so he was at Home Park deserve highlighting.

When it became obvious Ipswich were keen to sign him I urged the old board, as I still call them, to push the asking price as high as they could, which eventually led to the £2million mark.

Talk about January sales, eh?

Losing those key players was bad enough but what was to follow over the coming couple of seasons was even worse.

On, but more critically, off the pitch where decisions were made which affected not only my time at Argyle, but also ultimately led to the mess that saw Plymouth fall two divisions and into administration.

Now, I'll put my hands up straight away and admit that so far as signings were concerned, it's as if I'd been captured by aliens and the Paul Sturrock who prided himself on shrewd transfer dealings, had been replaced by someone who knew nothing about the game.

Consequently, the eye-catching signings or replacements for those who had gone that I made didn't work out and that was my fault.

Steve MacLean had been a 20-goal striker for me at Sheffield Wednesday only two years earlier but his cruciate knee injury had taken its toll and he had lost a yard of pace.

When Simon Walton arrived with his page 3 wife maybe I should have read the script then, added to which the boy had no real pace and was nothing like the player who had played for Leeds United as a 16-year-old.

Had I done my homework, I don't think either Steve or Simon would have been signed by Plymouth.

These boys' wages and contracts put a strain on the Argyle's player budget and when they didn't come off, it meant the players I'd also signed as squad players were having to step up to the first team, which hadn't been my intention.

But in mitigation, I was still struggling with my Parkinson's disease treatment and the balance of medicine and tablets I was taking wasn't working. So much so that I was listless and tired during the day and wide awake at night.

Not a great scenario but I was still trying to find the right balance for my health and manage a football club.

Furthermore I made a bad mistake in not letting on, particularly to Paul Stapleton, that I had Parkinson's, and it was only when it became obvious through the tell-tale signs of my physical appearance that I admitted publicly I had it.

These days, the tablets I'm taking are working well and although there is no cure for Parkinson's, I'm able to carry out my managerial duties perfectly well. My mind is as sharp as ever it was and my hunger for success just as keen.

But it was wrong of me not to have told the chairman that, yes, I did have Parkinson's at the outset and for that I'm sorry.

Towards the end of the 2007/08 campaign and in the lead-up to the 2008/09 season, the Plymouth Argyle board were in the process of negotiating a takeover with a consortium of Far East and Japanese businessmen, who said they had £3million to pump into the club.

I believe the idea was for Japanese players to come across and establish themselves in the English Football League. Unfortunately, if that was the case then they certainly hadn't boned up on the cross-border rules as foreign footballers have to be of a certain pedigree, and not younger players who didn't fit that criteria and consequently wouldn't get a work permit.

I remember having a chat with one of the delegation from the Far East and spelling out the realities, which didn't go down very well with the Shonan K&K Management Corporation or their British advisors.

That potential takeover and the situation the following year when Messrs Sir Roy Gardiner and Keith Todd joined the rush to buy into Plymouth Argyle and the dream of hosting World Cup matches turned what had been a well-run football club into the very opposite.

But returning to on-field football matters, without doubt the Emile Mpenza signing was probably the cherry on the parfait as far as misfiring captures is concerned.

I can only say in my defence that I was urged by the board to bring in a marquee signing for the 2008/09 Championship season.

The board wanted a £10,000-a-week player that would turn heads and show Argyle meant business and had ambition. Mpenza was the one we eventually ended up with.

Now Plymouth Argyle fans are among the most loyal and supportive in the country, but they must realise that geography and finance have always been major factors at the football club. Nevertheless, Belgian international Mpenza's signing in early September 2008 proved to be a disaster, both financially and effectively, as I think he played something like nine games and only scored a couple of goals.

The former Manchester City striker was paid off the following summer by which time he had hoovered up thousands of pounds in wages and set a new record in terms of excuses for injury absences.

I think the best one from Emile or his advisor, God knows I was losing the will to live let alone listen to his litany of misery, came when I asked the oft-repeated question, 'Has anyone seen the boy Mpenza?'

I was told, in all seriousness, that Emile had taken Viagra the previous night and still had an erection and wouldn't be able to take part in training.

The excuse has gone down in the annals of urban myth but I swear it's true. Even by football's standards of surreal moments, it is in a class of its own.

But just as serious and disappointing was the attitude of Marcel Seip, whose refusal to take his place on the substitutes' bench in a Championship match with Charlton was inexcusable in my view.

I had preferred Russell Anderson to play alongside Krisztian Timar in central defence for the Home Park clash on April 5, 2008, which we lost 2-1 and as a consequence valuable ground in the promotion play-off race.

I'd told Seip he'd be on the subs' bench and he said he was carrying an injury and wouldn't do it and stormed off. I was astonished as were the rest of the players, whom he had let down big time.

Anyway, I fined him two weeks' wages and told the board, which included his father-in-law, Paul Stapleton, that I wanted him sacked there and then.

But instead I found out that his mutiny had been rewarded with a new and vastly improved contract, some £6,000 a week, plus a loyalty bonus. I kid you not. Not only did the news put the cat among the pigeons with his team-mates, who quite naturally, wanted pay-rises, too, but it also undermined my standing in the eyes of the squad.

To my way of thinking the Seip incident was a microcosm of the malaise that was infecting Plymouth Argyle, and contributed to the club's downfall.

I'll be frank, when Seip refused to play, I saw it as a chance to replace him, as I felt he was too small to be effective as a centre-half and was better suited as a full-back.

That's a manager or coach's pragmatic assessment and wasn't based on anything other than how to improve the team's performances. I knew that the Seip–Timar pairing had been targeted by opposition managers as a potential weakness in the Argyle rearguard, which is the view I took.

Seip later apologised for his no-show, but so far as I and the team were concerned the damage had been done.

Seip's new contract was handled by director Robert Dennerly, as Stapleton was out of the country. I also seem to remember Stapleton's wages policy was that you didn't pay a defender as much as a striker.

In my view, Stapleton, who had done a commendable job as chairman previously, had blundered and left the manager he had appointed twice – namely me – in a weaker position than I merited.

Anyway, after claiming a top 10 position in 2007/08, the following season was a real battle to stay in the Championship. We survived by one place and five points better off than the relegated teams in 21st place.

Our leading goalscorer was on-loan Blackburn Rovers striker Paul Gallagher with a tally of 13 goals and Plymouth had enjoyed a day out in the capital with a third round FA Cup tie at Arsenal.

We lost 3-1 to Arsene Wenger's team, which was no disgrace, and at least the Green Army were able to enjoy a brief respite from the rigours of Championship survival.

To their immense credit, the fans stayed loyal to Argyle, in spite of the disappointing results and distractions of a potential takeover of the club, with us averaging nearly 12,000 at Home Park for the season.

In 2009/10, I stayed in charge until the board or rather executive director Keith Todd, who was now running the 'good ship Pilgrims' decided to promote Paul Mariner to the manager's post shortly before Christmas.

My final match was at Swansea on December 8, when we lost for the third league game in a row 1-0. However, the most controversial incident in my 19 rounds of that sorrowful season came at Bloomfield Road, on October 17, against Holloway's Blackpool, which has become better known as 'Thumbsgate'.

Argyle had just enjoyed back-to-back victories at Peterborough and Scunthorpe, respectively, and we went to the seaside reasonably optimistic of extending that unbeaten run or at best claiming a hat-trick of victories which would have eased the pressure on all concerned.

Seip had been loaned out to Blackpool and bizarrely had been allowed to play by Todd, which displayed the latter's naivety or complete lack of knowledge regarding football, as traditional wisdom dictates never to let an employee figure in a fixture between his current and previous teams.

And wouldn't you know it, that truism came back to bite Argyle in the rear end as Seip scored the first of Blackpool's goals after half-an-hour in what proved to be a 2-0 home victory.

The reaction of the Stapleton family, well leastways the Dutchman's mother-in-law Kim and wife, Lucy, caught on camera giving Seip the thumbs-up, was a gaffe which gave great offence not just to an Argyle team fighting for their lives, but the Green Army who had made the long journey to Lancashire at their own expense.

I didn't want Seip to play against us, but Todd said before and after the game that he didn't see what all the fuss was about or words to that effect.

But the players certainly did and in the next match at Home Park, captain Carl Fletcher celebrated his goal along with several of the players in the 1-1 draw with fellow strugglers Ipswich by giving the thumbs-up to the directors' box.

Anyway, Todd was a busy boy over the next couple of months, bringing in former Argyle old boy and England international Paul Mariner as head coach, with me as team manager, at Home Park.

Initially, Mariner, who had been based in North America for 20 years or so, had been persuaded by Todd to return to Plymouth as an ambassador for the city in their bid to be one of the host cities for England's 2018 World Cup.

Sloop and Summers were both relieved of their duties in October, with Mariner taking charge of their roles, while I soldiered on until Todd asked to speak to me.

I invited him around for a meal and drinks at my home and we made reasonably convivial small-talk until he informed me that I was sacked and would be replaced by Mariner.

I was stunned to say the least and told him that in all my years of football, being sacked from the manager's job by someone who has just enjoyed a good meal in my house takes the biscuit.

Or words to that effect, I may have told Todd to fuck off out of it, but it didn't matter as the damage had been done.

Argyle couldn't afford to sack me but asked if I would stay on in a commercial capacity, which I did.

As for Mariner, I'm afraid his appointment didn't have the hoped-for change in fortune Todd wanted and Argyle were relegated at the end of the season – to League One.

Nice man that Paul Mariner is, he had no concept of coaching and preparing teams in the English league.

At our first training session, I asked him if he would put together a back four while I would look after the forwards. Mariner said, sorry Paul I don't know how to do that, I've never been asked to do that and so never learned.

Really, in mine and many others' view the only board member to come out of the whole period with any personal integrity and honour intact, is Tony Wrathall, who lost a fortune trying to stem the flow of money and buy Plymouth time to sort out their affairs.

To me, Tony is a hero and his contribution to the cause of trying to save the club he loved deserves to be given its proper reward.

I used to tell him 'say no' whenever one of the board came asking for a cheque to cover some bill or other, but Tony would always stump up.

Tony is back on the Plymouth Argyle board again now under their chairman James Brent and the

club and supporters are lucky to have such a good
bloke and genuine fan working in their interests.

So, looking back, a number of mistakes were
made and I made my share to which I've owned up,
but that was small beer compared to the financial
mismanagement of a once well-run club which
almost put Plymouth Argyle out of business.

As for me, well there's always the next game
to look forward to and, from Dundee United, St
Johnstone, Plymouth, Southampton, Sheffield
Wednesday, Swindon and Southend to where I am
at the time writing this book, Yeovil Town, the song
remains the same.

* * * * *

JOHN BLACKLEY had no reservations, at first,
about following Paul Sturrock back to Plymouth
Argyle. After all, Home Park had been the scene
of great success for the two Scots and Kevin
Summerfield.

But Blackley sensed a different atmosphere
prevailed in the 2007/08 season as he explained:

*Things had changed, people had changed and you didn't
get the same feedback from the powers in charge, who*

were basically the same people as when we'd left them. But it was different this time around, the club seemed to have gone into decline from what it had been. The chairman, Paul Stapleton, was still there as were a few others from before, but the whole ambience was different. The Plymouth we had left was a well-oiled machine and run in an orderly fashion. Before the board members had been relaxed and allowed Paul to make the decisions a manager should make. It seemed to me that they had their own thoughts about how the club should be run and as events proved, they blew it.

Perhaps, you could say that they had got too big for their boots, but whatever description you care to choose, things were not the same for a football management team.

✳ ✳ ✳ ✳ ✳

KEVIN SUMMERFIELD remains philosophical over how things worked out at Plymouth and said:

In retrospect I don't think it was the wisest decision we made – they say don't go back, don't they? But we were all together, Paul, Sloop and myself and that was important. Also we all came out of it the other end to fight another day at another football club.

For me it was Tranmere who rang me up out of the blue after the longest break I think I'd had in football and I became assistant manager to Les Parry in July 2010 and then Gary Rowett at Burton and now Birmingham City.

But I never worked with Paul Sturrock again, although, naturally, I've followed his progress with Southend United and now at Yeovil Town. And we've bumped into one another from time to time.

If anything now Paul is looking a hell of a lot better than he was a few years back, he did a great job with Southend – he is dealing with his illness and has proved he has his wits about him.

Chairman Has His Say

P AUL STAPLETON, former Plymouth Argyle chairman, recalls the ultimately disappointing second coming of Sturrock and in a frank interview also gives his version of affairs both on and off the pitch. He said:

When we were hit by Ian Holloway's sudden departure in November 2007, Argyle were in seventh place in the Championship – we moved to fourth the following Saturday winning 1-0 at Sheffield United and we were very keen as a board to keep the good times going.

We had reached the quarter-final of the FA Cup earlier in the year and were now riding high in the

Championship. We arranged a board meeting for the morning of the Sheffield game in the team hotel.

Although Phill Gill had taken it on himself to talk to two potential managers during the week the meeting decided unanimously to approach Swindon for permission to speak to Paul.

We had had great times with Paul up to 2004 and since leaving (and ignoring Southampton) he had had success at both Sheffield Wednesday and at Swindon. In fact, I had kept in regular contact with Paul, meeting him when up north for a meal and going to Sheffield for his 50th birthday party at Hillsborough. It proved to be an enjoyable evening with Guy Branston for company.

I knew Paul was keen to come back thinking there was unfinished business. Indeed one of his close Plymouth friends often told me Paul would walk back to Plymouth for the job.

I think Paul missed Plymouth, the city and a lot of the friends he had made here.

The board agreed they wanted a manager who we could trust to look after the club's money like it was his own and someone who had had success in his career. We also wanted someone to come in sooner rather than later as we wanted to keep the momentum going.

Swindon gave permission and compensation was agreed.

I didn't know about Paul's condition until a year later which was a strange affair as I had asked him whether he had the illness after reading about the condition in the paper and he had said no.

Paul had to come in when our players – Norris, Ebanks-Blake, Hayles, Gosling – were being poached by other clubs. Because we were playing so well other clubs were looking at why we were near the top.

So when January came we were losing key players but we as a board backed Paul with transfer and loan fees.

A record fee for Steve MacLean of £500,000, fees of £200,000 for Clark and Paterson, in addition to loan fees for Anderson and Teale etc. The transfer fees received were put back into paying fees and wages to try to maintain our push for promotion.

We were well in contention until the last four games and one point from two home games sealed our fate and we came 10th – our highest finish for many a year.

The next season saw the Japanese come in and more movement of players with Halmosi out and players like Mpenza, Marin and Gallagher in. We struggled that season but avoided relegation with the win at champions Wolves in March 2009 the game that pushed us to safety.

That summer saw new control at the club with Keith Todd and Sir Roy Gardiner having control using the Japanese shares to gain 51% ownership. Todd took control with Gardiner as chairman and I, having been chairman since 2001, found I had little say and no longer had the cheque book.

My reign had come to an end, I was not in control of decision making any more, in fact, Todd referred to me as an irritant according to an inside source.

Paul had to forge a relationship with Keith Todd and our relationship suffered.

Keith Todd had subsequently made contact with Paul Mariner, saying his meal out with him was like going on a first date, and pushed to bring him in as Paul Sturrock's assistant. This ultimately happened and when results suffered Paul was moved upstairs and Paul Mariner appointed head coach.

This was not a unanimous decision but as they had control it happened.

Sadly, relegation followed and the downward spiral continued. The World Cup bid had been a massive and costly distraction, too.

How we longed for the simple days of 2001 to 2004!

Paul's second period had not been the success we had hoped for but there were different circumstances. Starting with players coming and going, the Japanese coming in with unfulfilled promises followed by the New World promises of Todd and Gardiner.

It was not the stable environment we had in our successful years.

Stapleton was equally forthright on the sad sagas of two failed takeover bids. The Japanese through Mr Kagami`s company K and K consortium bought shares in April 2008 to have a 20% stake in the club.

Mr Kagami became a director but his associate Tony Campbell acted on his behalf in board meetings.

The promise of £3m was a commercial deal signed by the club with a cut-off date of 8/8/08. The £3m never came although Tony Campbell insisted it would come, even subsequently promising £1m personally from Mr Kagami by the end of November 2008. Mr Kagami was listed as being worth £45m in the Japanese rich list so apparently there was no issue with the funds EXCEPT they never came!

Ironically, in March 2009, they paid Phill Gill over £600k for his shares in the club so they found the money for that.

It was this promise of money which persuaded Paul to bring in Marin (didn't work out), Mpenza (didn't work out) and Paul Gallagher (thank goodness as he kept us up).

I had never spent money we didn't have so to spend on this guaranteed promise was taken in the utmost good faith. Tony Campbell was adamant it was coming. The minutes of our board meetings confirm this.

You may note that when Todd and Gardiner took over they joined with the Japanese to have 51% of the club and control and even after that the Japanese still promised funds to them which didn't materialise.

Yes, it is a pity that we ever got involved with them but no I don't blame myself as we were all equal on the board and all made the collective decision. Indeed Kagami came to visit and displayed ambition although it is true to say that his wish to have a Japanese player playing for the club never materialised for a number of reasons. This didn't help the relationship.

Finally Tony Campbell was a very persuasive person assuring us of his relationship with Kagami and that he was a very honourable man.

I have a slightly different story to Paul regarding Marcel Seip walking out of the dressing room before the Charlton game.

Marcel was playing through a double hernia problem, taking 15 tablets every time he played to get him through the games. He told me that he had told the manager that if his performance was affected because of his injury or indeed if he wanted to change personnel then to tell him and he would understand and look to have an operation.

Just before the game Marcel had got ready as usual, had taken his tablets when Paul told him he was sub. This according to Marcel was not the agreement so he asked to have a private word, Paul said see me on Monday. After a few more requests to discuss with the same answer, Marcel walked out.

When the dust had settled Paul put Marcel on the transfer list and Marcel went to Holland for the operation on his groin. I agreed with Paul that Marcel should not have walked out even with his extenuating circumstances and Marcel was duly fined.

I do not recall Paul saying to me he wanted to sack him.

Nothing was said about Marcel until the new season when Paul told the board that the only way Marcel could come back in the fold was if he sincerely apologised to the manager and the players and that his commitment on and off the field would be monitored for the first 10 games.

Indeed Marcel was outstanding on the field, eventually finishing runner-up to Romain Larrieu in the player of the year vote such that Paul asked the board to give him a new contract rising to £5,000 from £3,000 per week.

LUGGY

In the period from April to October 2008 when the new offer was made Halmosi was being offered £5,500 per week, Timar (June) had been renegotiated to £5,000 per week, Walton signed at that and Gallagher (September) at £6,000 per week and of course Mpenza was on £10,000 per week.

Therefore, factually, Marcel wasn't the start of the high wages syndrome. As for the Blackpool situation this should never have arisen.

Ian Holloway, who liked Marcel's play asked for him on loan and Todd said yes, allowing him to play against us.

However, the worst thing was the photo of my wife putting her thumbs up to Marcel at the end of the game was leaked to the press, I think by Todd to undermine me.

If you look at the photo I am not celebrating or putting my thumbs up. I am looking bemused because my team has lost. My wife is congratulating her son-in-law on a fine game.

The leaking of the photo and its publication at the same time as my wife was on the front page for a fatal road accident was insensitive and very callous to say the least. I should have left the board then but I couldn't prove anything. The players reacted in the next game but I took that as a gesture to the board for letting Marcel play. Mickey Mouse, Carl Fletcher called it.

* * * * *

TONY WRATHALL, former and now current Plymouth Argyle director added his thoughts on the times regarding the second reign of Paul Sturrock. He said:

It was Paul Stapleton who pressed the case for Paul Sturrock to return as manager of Plymouth Argyle.

I hadn't been a board member during Paul's first spell as manager but as a fan knew that Paul had been fantastic. I had joined in 2005 when Bobby Williamson was the Argyle manager, in succession to Luggy.

Anyway, when Ian Holloway left for Leicester City, me and everyone else at the club were keen to make an appointment as soon as possible. I remember there were four of us in the room when Paul Stapleton suggested Paul Sturrock be appointed, but it wasn't unanimous, as I abstained from the vote.

I think someone else said no, or they weren't sure, but as chairman, Paul Stapleton had the casting vote and said he would seek permission to interview Paul from his Swindon counterpart. And the deal was agreed and Paul returned as boss in late November 2007.

As for the sequence of events which led to the eventual collapse of two potential takeovers and two relegations and the club going into administration in 2011, I can confirm that serious mistakes were made which eventually led to me losing £2.1million, personally, and my health suffering badly in the process.

We should never have allowed the Japanese consortium to miss a deadline to put the promised money into the club in 2008 and should have learned from the lesson when the same thing happened when Roy Gardiner and Keith Todd and the Japanese took a controlling interest of 51% the following summer.

With no money coming in from our potential backers, I was being put under pressure to cover the costs from my own pocket, on the promise that the monies would be paid back.

They never were.

The largest amount I was asked to give the club came on the eve of the open-air Rod Stewart concert on July 2 at Home Park. The board asked me to put up £500,000 and I would get back the money once the gig was over. I asked what happens if I don't stump up the money and was told that no dough meant no show, as Rod Stewart wanted the money, in dollars, up front and that I'd get my money back on the day of the concert.

Well, Todd and Gardiner came into the frame, the day before Rod Stewart and the World Cup bid started and they asked me if I would leave the money to cover the July and August wages and they would pay me back later.

But it never happened, they never paid me back.

Todd said that if I left the money in, then I could stay on the board and Paul Stapleton and Rob Dennerly would be going as soon as they could pay them off. I was told Sir Roy would pay me back the £500,000. I believe that Gardiner was a figurehead or sleeping partner, call it what you will, and that Todd was calling the shots.

Sir Roy had come to us with a great CV of running companies and was a former Manchester United PLC chairman, but we never saw much of him at Home Park. And I don't think he knew what was going on.

I was continually being asked for a £100,000 here and there to tide the club over which I did even after Paul Sturrock had gone and been replaced in the short term by Paul Mariner.

I remember one particular day in the October before we went into administration in 2011, Todd collared me in the car park and said Tony can I have a word. I said OK and he said we've got cash problems and unless someone can put in £150,000 into the club by Friday, we'll have to call in the administrators. He said Roy will give it to you back, he'll sort you out.

So, I agreed to lend the club another £150,000, but Roy and Keith never said a word about it and I never saw the money. I had an argument with Gardiner, accusing him of not knowing what was going on at the club of which he was chairman. It was a real messy period to say the least.

Peter Ridsdale, formerly of Leeds and Cardiff, was brought in as a football consultant and was going over the books trying to find out what was going on and he went public at the end of February claiming there was no money left in the accounts to pay the staff.

Well you know the rest, Argyle went into administration at the start of March 2011, had been docked 10 points and were all set for a struggle in League Two – just to stay in the Football League set-up.

James Brent took over as owner later in 2011 and has brought stability back to a club which once had it and then lost it, but now is moving forward purposefully again.

Personally, the whole situation left me a lot poorer financially and almost ruined my health through worry and put my family through a terrible period of anxiety. I thought long and hard before agreeing to James Brent's invitation for me to return to the board, which I did in March 2014, almost three years to the day I left.

There are a lot of nice people at Plymouth and once you're a fan of a club, you just want to do everything in your power to help them move forward. But I took five or six months over the winter of 2013 before I was finally persuaded to take up James's offer and return to Home Park. At the end of the day I just wanted to put right what had gone wrong.

The day I returned for a football match at Home Park, was the greatest and most emotional day of my life on the board of Plymouth Argyle. I was so nervous and apprehensive and felt sick at the prospect but the welcome I received was fantastic. It took about two hours for me to cross the car park to the boardroom and Argyle beat Morecambe 5-0, to set the seal on a marvellous day.

Southend United
2010–13

THE offer to manage Southend United came along just at the right time for me as I'd been twiddling my thumbs for long enough since leaving Plymouth in the April of 2010. If a week in politics is a long time, as Harold Wilson famously said, then I can confirm that around 10 weeks out of football management feels like an eternity.

I went up to London to meet Southend's chairman, Ron Martin, whom I'd had conversations with whenever one of my teams were playing his side.

It's ironic, that whenever I went to Southend, I always ended up in the manager's office for one reason or another. But the fact is I half-knew Ron and was comfortable in his company.

Anyway, cutting to the chase, someone who knew both of us recommended me to Ron, who looked at my CV and then offered me the job.

I inherited a fellow called Tommy Widdrington as my assistant manager, as a condition of me taking up the appointment.

Tommy had managed Salisbury City and was a kind of up-and-at-'em sort of fellow and very keen. I think Southend wanted him there alongside me in case my health became an issue, or I struggled because of my age, then he would step in.

The trouble with Tommy was he alienated players with his comments and his demeanour and, in fact, I had a mini-revolt on my hands because of his manner.

There were rumours that Tommy wasn't happy with my son, Blair, playing and with some of my tactics and training schedules.

Graham Coughlan had joined me as a player and was becoming more and more influential on the training ground. Cocko, as Graham is known, had been with me at Plymouth and also at Sheffield Wednesday, where he was named their player of the season the year after I left.

Anyway, I was between a rock and a hard place as some of the senior pros came to see me and told me they were disgruntled with Tommy. Also finances were a big issue at Southend as basically the club was on its haunches.

So, financially, it also made sense for Tommy to go, particularly as I had a delegation of players coming in to see me complaining about Tommy and he left just before Christmas that same year. Cocko stepped up to the mark and became player-coach.

But prior to that, in the July, I faced the onerous task of trying to find players to play in friendly matches, as at one stage we only had a handful of first-team footballers on the books to call upon.

The players hadn't been paid in a long spell and officially over three months and on my first training session, several of them informed me that they were going to hand in a letter of resignation, which as unpaid employees, they were entitled to do.

So one morning, five of the nine players on the books came to me with their letters of resignation and told me they were leaving.

Therefore, when I went back to my hotel in the afternoon, I was left with just four players with which to start the season, and the 2010/11 campaign, which was getting closer and closer.

It was either laugh or cry time and I just started giggling then laughing aloud to myself – people must have thought I'd gone mad.

But it was the enormity of the situation and I didn't know there was an embargo on recruitment, so I had to go down the route of holding trial games, to see if we could swell the ranks.

It was a case of beg, steal and borrow and something I'd never had to deal with before, despite my fire-fighting reputation.

But I've always relished a challenge and from some of the games, I recruited Bilel Moshni, Lee Sawyer and Ryan Hall, who'd all done very well. So, with Cocko, Anthony Grant, Blair, Barry Corr, Craig Easton and Chris Barker, we had the semblance of a squad.

But not enough players to fulfil a pre-season friendly as I tried to tell Ipswich Town manager Roy Keane, who was not at all impressed or sympathetic to my predicament.

Roy took terrible umbrage on the phone, insisting the game must go ahead and that I had a youth squad and must play the youngsters against his senior side, which I had no intention of doing.

Looking back it's all very funny, but, Roy wasn't a happy bunny when I forced the issue and had to cancel the game. Anyway, we had a pre-season friendly against Dartford with my Southend side packed full of trialists, apart from the four players who were registered.

At the same time as I was trying to get rid of players and sign others as a matter of urgency.

But someone at the club said I couldn't register new recruits as it was against Football League rules, as we hadn't paid players we already had on the books. There were certain bills at the club that hadn't been paid either which put a freeze on any future recruits.

So, I had the unenviable task of going up to the 12 or 13 players I'd offered contracts to and who had signed on, and telling them that the agreements weren't valid and they weren't registered and wouldn't be until the club had settled outstanding debts.

I don't know what I expected from the boys but I was so proud that all the lads who I'd had to let down, turned up for training even though there was no guarantee of a job for them.

I can't speak highly enough of those boys.

But it meant we had to play a smattering of pre-season games with a mix and match line-up of those players on the books, those hoping to join and youth players. Anyway on the pre-match Friday and just before the training session, chairman Ron came down to the ground early and told me all the bills had been paid and we could register the players in time for Saturday's season opener.

Our League Two game, and my first as manager for a competitive clash, was at home to Stockport, who had been relegated with us, and despite the players not really knowing one another, we managed a 1-1 draw. But it was a close-run affair, as we had been losing 1-0 until Blair scored with a header, from a corner, two minutes from time.

Our next match was a Carling Cup tie with Bristol City, also at Roots Hall, which we won 3-2.

So despite the unpromising start to life at Southend, by the end of the 2010/11 season we had consolidated our place in the division and finished in mid-table.

The following season we decided to have a right go at promotion and amassed 83 points, but missed out by one point to the third automatic promotion place held by Crawley.

It was the first time that a team had finished with that many points and not gone up.

We were gutted, but it was a terrific effort by everyone concerned.

But we did qualify for the promotion semi-finals where we were pitted against Crewe Alexandra, who finished seventh to claim the final play-off place.

However, we were knocked out of the play-offs by Crewe 3-2 on aggregate after two tough legs.

I think injuries and suspensions had caught up with us but we'd ended up in a top-four place, agonisingly close to a return to League One.

Interestingly and unusually, our top scorer in the league that season was Bilel Moshni, one of the trialists we'd taken on and who had played all his career at centre-back and was an imposing figure.

Bilel had a wee altercation with an Orient player in a League Cup tie and after the game ran down the tunnel to the physio's office and grabbed a pair of scissors and tried to get into the away changing room.

It took four players to hold him down, while the Orient players changed and went away on the bus.

Anyway, rather than letting him go, I tried to channel his aggression by getting him involved in cage fighting by contacting one of the lads I knew in Southend and asked him if he could teach Bilel the rudimentary rules of the sport.

Many a day he came back with a black eye and a bloody nose which seemed to work for a while, but his discipline on the pitch was always an issue, given that he was playing centre-back and having to make tackles which sometimes sparked into something worse.

Anyway, one day, I decided to put him on the left wing where he wouldn't get so involved and it proved to be a shrewd move as he became an influential player for us, scoring and making loads of goals in that season.

I stood by Bilel and I'm glad, as a nicer lad on a day-to-day basis you'll never meet until the whistle went on a Saturday and he became a different person altogether.

And another lad I'd brought to the club, Ryan Hall, had a problem and was jailed for hitting a lad at a Christmas party, an event which was caught on CCTV. Ryan had also been handed an eight-game ban, and I took him back, although other managers would have sacked him.

Ryan, though, was a character and a half and his disciplinary record always let him down.

Fergie said to me 'leopards never change their spots' and I've been trying for years to prove him wrong.

But I must admit he's right as sooner or later the leopard and his spots will re-emerge.

The following season was about getting over the disappointment of missing out on promotion and building up for a push in what was my third term in charge – 2012/13.

And it turned out, it was to be my final one as manager of Southend United, as both myself and Andrea, my partner, had decided we wanted to be back in the south-west, and Cornwall.

So, I had that in my mind but also the thoughts that Southend were not far away from being serious promotion prospects, as we had proved the previous season.

We had some attractive pre-season friendlies, including West Ham United and Spurs, and began the term with two defeats and a draw before scoring our first victory on September 1 against Wycombe at home. We went on a bit of a run then, winning three out of four and claiming a draw with Plymouth at Home Park.

It was that kind of campaign, but nothing as impressive as the season before, league position-wise and I believe Southend ended up in 11th place, but I'd gone by then, having been sacked towards the end of March. I feel that chairman Ron had been thinking for some time that a new manager would revive the players.

The highlight for Southend was reaching the final of the Johnstone's Paint Trophy to be played at Wembley.

I was offered the chance of leading the players out at Wembley, but I didn't think it appropriate, although the decision to ask me was popular with the fans and many of the players. The lads had put together two great performances against Leyton Orient and Southend won 3-2 on aggregate to go to the final.

Southend lost to Crewe 2-0 in the early April final, but the foundation built by myself, Cocko and those loyal players two years earlier, was well and truly set in place.

* * * * *

Irishman GRAHAM COUGHLAN, who is still at the Essex outfit, said:

Paul joined Southend in 2010 and I joined him in Essex firstly as a reserve-team manager and player and then he gave me my first chance in management as a first-team coach.

It was a great experience for me and very hard going but Paul again showed his trust in me and handed over the coaching duties to me and allowed me to implement my own ideas and stamp my own authority.

I believe Paul's achievement in managing Southend and stabilising the club cannot be overstated.

Because of the financial constraints and embargoes on the club, we only had three or four players who were going to stay and a few players had handed in their two-weeks' notices, as they were entitled to do.

So effectively, in real terms, we had no players going into the 2010/11 League Two season, in fact we went three or four weeks in pre-season without actually registering a player.

Recruitment wasn't a problem at Southend, as we had players, many of whom were of a very good quality, trouble was because of the transfer embargo, we couldn't sign any of them.

Added to which the staff at Roots Hall weren't getting paid either and they all left – so it was not an ideal situation, but Paul said 'it is a man's job and it needs doing'.

We had to beg, borrow and steal to get a team on the pitch and mostly through Paul's contacts in the game, we were able to gradually freshen up and strengthen Southend.

So, to come out of that 'scary scenario' as Paul would describe it later, and survive that first season and in the next one get very close to promotion, was an incredible achievement and must rank high among even Paul's brilliant successes.

I know I'm enormously proud of what we managed to do and had we more bodies from which to choose, I'm convinced Southend would have made the play-offs in 2010/11.

It meant an awful lot of hard work on the training ground and driving mile upon mile scouting for new players by just the three of us on the coaching staff, helped to keep Southend in the Football League. And I'm convinced that helped to lay the foundations for what Southend have recently achieved, notably our promotion via the play-offs in the 2014/15 season.

I was very, very proud to lead out Southend United in the JPT Final at Wembley in 2013, after Paul had been sacked.

Paul's dismissal hit us all very hard and although he was offered the opportunity of leading United in the JPT Final against Crewe, he turned it down and I took his place in Paul's honour.

Tribute To Andy King

I HAVE met more good people than the other sort during my footballing career, and one of the best was Andy King, who died from a heart attack at the end of May, aged just 58.

Andy had a glittering football career as a midfielder which took him from his hometown club, Luton, on to Everton (twice), and West Brom and he was a skilful and infectiously cheerful player.

I was aware of Andy's reputation as a player and although roughly the same age, our paths crossed not on the pitch but on the managerial circuit.

Andy was manager of Swindon while I was at Plymouth and our teams had a few tussles as did we, verbally, from opposing dug-outs. It was all good-natured banter and Andy was terrifically fast on the repartee, probably the most quick-witted bloke I have met.

In one of those quirks of fortune when Andy was sacked I would later become a manager at Swindon and we went on to become firm friends.

I would phone Andy and ask him if he would mind giving me some background on the situation at Swindon and if he would give me a few pointers.

Periodically, Andy would come to some of the games at Swindon and we would get chatting about this and that. When I went back to Plymouth I contacted Andy again about scouting for us, as I knew he'd done a similar job at Sunderland and knew how to spot a player.

In footballing terms, he had a great manner about him and was knowledgeable about the game.

At that time Andy was unemployed and working in his sister's pub in Luton, and so he was delighted to get that job.

We got more and more friendly and there was a phone call near enough every day and we visited one another so our friendship blossomed.

He was a delight to be with and I've never met a funnier man in my life, he had a razor-sharp wit and best of all he loved life. And although he'd had a heart attack before in 2009 it was such a shock when his wife Barbara told me that he'd had another and had died.

He'd had a fitness regime, took tablets and fought a long battle to keep himself healthy.

I went to his funeral in Liverpool and you could tell just how well thought of Andy was, as there were hundreds of Everton fans outside the church. The fans lined the route and applauded Andy's hearse, it was a very, very moving moment.

Andy's former team-mates and friends in the game, Peter Reid, Graeme Sharp, Kevin Ratcliffe, Andy Gray and Mick Harford were in attendance, with the latter reading out a heartfelt tribute to his old mate.

It was amazing to see how many lives Andy had touched and was one of those sad days for me as I'd also lost a good friend.

Andy King will be well missed.

My Three Trusty Lieutenants

I COUNT myself as being extremely fortunate to have had coaching staff I could rely upon during my managerial career.

Without exception Graham Coughlan, John 'Sloop' Blackley and Kevin Summerfield have all supported and remained loyal to me, often in trying circumstances, in the rollercoaster ride that comes with being a football manager.

Without coaches you can trust and respect and who can read off the same hymn sheet as yourself, becoming a successful and promotion-winning manager is all but impossible. I brought in Graham Coughlan at Southend United as a player to start with a wee promise that he could help me with the coaching duties.

Graham or Cocko as we all know him was coming to the end of his playing career and as a no-nonsense centre-back with me at Plymouth and Sheffield Wednesday had natural leadership qualities and a winning mentality.

He is a dedicated professional and really wants to do well and I'm convinced he has a glittering career in management still to come.

Graham is at the stage now that he needs to start picking up a manager's job.

He is very thorough in his approach and I must admit I was delighted to show him the ropes and start him along the road of management.

Graham has the personality, character and the will to win and is also a strict disciplinarian as well, so I'm expecting him to reach the heights.

I had no doubts over his commitment to the cause.

Graham showed that when he came down to Plymouth as a player from Livingston and signed the papers the same day and went back up to Scotland to prepare for life in the West Country.

He hadn't even seen Plymouth as a place to live but trusted me enough to believe in what I was looking to achieve and we have formed a good working relationship ever since.

Just as I couldn't write a book without a tribute to Graham, nor could I omit a reference to the debt of gratitude I owe both John Blackley and Kevin Summerfield.

How I hired John is a funny one because when I became manager of St Johnstone I asked Jim McLean if I could have Gordon Wallace and was asked not to approach Gordon as he was needed at Dundee United. I didn't want to upset Dundee United's plans so I didn't push to have Gordon, and I next turned to Eamonn Bannon but he was tied up at Hearts in a coaching role at the time and couldn't come to McDiarmid Park.

And then, I remembered when I was taking my B Licence at the SFA's coaching course, that John was there at the same time as me and I remember being impressed after watching a couple of the sessions he ran.

His work on defensive duties particularly caught the eye and I knew someone of his ability would be invaluable at St Johnstone. John was working for the community in Falkirk but coaching below the standards he had achieved and should be concentrating on.

I was straight with John and told him that he hadn't been my first choice, but I can assure you it was the best decision I ever made.

Defensively, at any club I was at, John ensured I had a very strong and organised unit. It is John's specialist subject, defence, and as coach he can be strong, can be soft, players loved him and he had a dry humour and would crack a joke or two with the lads.

He offered the same level of professionalism and loyalty whether we were together at St Johnstone, Dundee United, Plymouth Argyle, Sheffield Wednesday, Swindon and back to Plymouth again.

Unfortunately, he didn't come to Southampton but I'm convinced he would have done the same great job there, too.

Kev was at Plymouth as a caretaker manager when I first arrived in 2000 but his main role had been as youth coach at Argyle and worked very hard with them.

I made a pact with Kev that after three months if he liked me and I liked him, then he could move up to the assistant manager's role.

He is without doubt a fantastic coach and a completely different character than say me or Sloop with a dry humour once you get to know him.

Kev's relationship with players could be rocky at times but he never backed down on what he felt was right and showed he had a strong character and you knew where you stood with him.

He was well respected by the players, not just for his straight-shooting style but also with what he was teaching them in his coaching sessions. They knew he was a good coach and he's gone on to prove that at Burton Albion and now Birmingham City.

Kev has made it plain that the role he fulfils as assistant manager is his niche and he has no aspirations to move into the hot seat.

He has excelled in that post and I'm very surprised that no-one has offered him another bite of the cherry in the Premier League for that's the standards he can achieve.

So, Sloop and Kev must take an awful lot of the credit and accolades for what I have achieved and all that's followed on from the promotions.

There's no ifs, buts or maybes, those two were a big part of it and I would like to thank both of them because I wouldn't have achieved as much under my name.

They also knew I had Parkinson's and kept their counsel and their help and discretion in keeping my secret is much appreciated.

LUGGY

It must have been very difficult for them with me in the second spell at Plymouth because the tablets I was on weren't working properly and I knew that both Kev and Sloop were disenchanted with me and I couldn't blame them.

And I judge both of them as my friends.

Parkinson's

LIVING with Parkinson's disease is not an easy ride as up to press there's no cure but there is medication you can take to ease the symptoms.

I know that I will get worse as I get older and that is why I am determined to live each day as if it is my last.

I was disappointed to read that a former Dundee United centre-forward Finn Dossing (Jensen) is a fellow sufferer and made a lot of comments about it which basically boiled down to 'why me?'

I think you have to be positive over Parkinson's, especially once you find out you can't die from it but you'll die with it and it won't go away but get worse.

So, that's why I believe it is important to enjoy life and not as Finn seems to be doing, looking at it negatively.

The right balance of tablets is such a key thing about Parkinson's and the story about me picking up a cup, seeing I had a shake and going to the club doctor at Plymouth who recommended that I see a specialist and me finding out I had the illness was a real shock.

Worrying about the dying side to the illness was the first thing that came to me and reading all about it was horrible.

I would recommend to anybody who has the early stages of Parkinson's not to read anything as it's a horror story and you'll feel suicidal, Believe me, I know, I've been there.

At the end of the day, you've just got to put it out of your mind – some days I forget to take my tablets because I'm so concentrated on living one day at a time. I've worked very hard to raise the profile of Parkinson's at different events both in the West Country and in London and I'm going to do more.

I've had to live with Parkinson's since just before I left for Southampton which is over a decade ago and I'm still here earning a living as a football manager with all the stress that goes with the job.

PARKINSONS

I had been out of the game for about two years when I took over the manager's role at Yeovil Town, who have had back-to-back relegations from the Championship to League Two, necessitating a massive clear-out and rebuild at Huish Park.

Sound familiar?